"I want to look back and have the exuberance for life that he had. I'll never forget it. Everyday you think about it and I honestly can say I can't think of anything other than the fun times with Greg. I look at all the young guys out there today trying to make this a career, and I see that they model themselves after Greg. They model themselves on how he behaved, how he enjoyed himself, on how he handled and conducted himself, and that's the greatest tribute." Mark Thorne

GREG MOORE
A LEGACY OF SPIRIT

FOREWORD BY JACQUES VILLENEUVE

BY DAN PROUDFOOT & GORDON KIRBY

WITH JIM TAYLOR

A WHITECAP/INSPERO BOOK

For Greg,
in loving memory.
See you at the front.

Published and produced by Inspero Productions Inc. West Vancouver, British Columbia, Canada

Published in Canada by Whitecap Books Ltd., 351 Lynn Avenue, North Vancouver, British Columbia, Canada V7J 2C4
www.whitecap.ca

First Published in 2000

10 9 8 7 6 5 4 3 2 1

Canadian Cataloguing in Publication Data
Proudfoot, Dan
 Greg Moore

 Includes index.
 ISBN 1-55285-139-7

 1. Moore, Greg, 1975-1999. 2. Automobile racing drivers--
 Canada--Biography. I. Kirby, Gordon. II. Title.
 GV1032.M55P76 2000   796.72'092   C00-910544-1

Design: CDDC Strategic Communications Inc.

Printed and bound in Canada
by Friesens Corporation

TABLE *of* CONTENTS

The Player's/Forsythe Racing Team.

A book about Greg Moore must be more about relationships than races. Greg Moore lived for the races, but wherever the sport took him, he never left his friends.

His greatest friend through childhood, adolescence, ascendance through the racing ranks, and into adulthood was his father Ric. The rare interaction between father and son will never be forgotten by those drivers against whom he competed so fiercely, or those friends in Maple Ridge, British Columbia, to whom he remained so loyal. Their relationship was the rock from which Greg Moore viewed the world. Commitment and consistency marked his business dealings and his personal friendships.

"If you had the pleasure of meeting Greg or watching him on the race track, you will never forget him," said Gerald Forsythe, owner of the Player's/Forsythe team. "This book will tell of his life to future racing enthusiasts around the world."

Don Brown, chairman and chief executive officer of Imperial Tobacco, Ltd., provided Moore with his pivotal break in the form of the Player's backing that brought him to Forsythe for the record-setting 1995 PPG-Firestone Indy Lights season. "Greg's performance, I think, really spoke for itself and assured his move into CART," Brown remembered about Greg's winning 10 of 12 Lights races in 1995.

Relationships. To those who knew him best, they're as central to his story as his daring pass of Alex Zanardi at Rio de Janeiro, his foot-to-the-floor spin at 230 miles-per-hour at

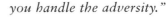

Michigan Speedway, or his crossing the finish line backwards at Motegi, Japan.

Al Speyer, Firestone director of motor sports, remembered the 1999 race in Japan as a time Moore could have blamed his tires, but didn't. "What I really remember about Greg's character is that after that difficulty on the re-start, he spun around, and went across the start-finish line backwards because there was no tread left on the rear tires," Speyer said.

"Here was the guy that had just lost a major race because the tires went over, and typical of Greg he said, 'Guys, don't worry about it. You've done a fine job. You've always been there for me. You know, racing has its ups and downs. And don't worry about it.' But that's what makes a really true champion, adversity and how you handle the adversity."

Steve Potter, Supervisor of Sports Marketing for Mercedes-Benz USA, recalls an athlete who never let his competitive nature overwhelm his human quality. "Greg wanted to win with every fiber of his being," Potter said. "But what made Greg mean so much to Mercedes was his ability to be driven to win without limit and without ever sacrificing being a decent person."

Greg Moore was the U.S. Formula 2000 champion in 1992 and the PPG-Firestone Indy Lights champion in 1995. Larger championships were in his future when he died October 31, 1999, at California Speedway, Fontana, California.

The Greg Moore Foundation, a charitable organization committed to helping young athletes achieve their potential, was founded by his father, step-mother Donna and friends to perpetuate his spirit. Net proceeds from this book, as well as from annual golf tournaments at his home races at Vancouver and Toronto, will help fund the Foundation.

DON BROWN	**GERALD FORSYTHE**	**STEVE POTTER**	**AL SPEYER**
Imperial Tobacco, Ltd.	*Player's/Forsythe*	*Mercedes-Benz, USA*	*Bridgestone/Firestone*

Jacques Villeneuve and Greg Moore, 1995.

FOREWORD

I did not have the pleasure of knowing Greg for very long, but like his quick rise to the top of motor racing, it didn't take long for him to leave a good, strong and lasting impression. His generous and friendly personality did not give you any choice: you had to like him.

You all know his racing exploits, how he thrived on the edge and pushed the limit, happily. You could imagine him driving with a grin.

In November 1998, Greg traveled with Jimmy Vasser and Dario Franchitti to join Mika Salo, Johnny Herbert, myself, and a few others in Helsinki, Finland, to participate in a Go-Kart Exhibition. It turned into a "Spring Break" weekend very quickly! We did a little bit of driving, a little bit of sleeping (mostly between driving stints) and a lot of having a good time.

Even though racing had matured Greg quite quickly, he hadn't discarded his youth and, during that particular weekend, with the partying, the joking, the tricks, it felt like we were all back at college. For most of us, it was our first days ever at college.

From that weekend, I was charmed by Greg and was eagerly awaiting the November '99 reunion in Las Vegas. We had the reunion, but in Greg's memory.

JACQUES VILLENEUVE

PUP
...EY TOURNAME...
1985

GREG

Moore is made for racing

He's 11 years old and looks nothing like Mario Andretti.
But Greg Moore comes from good racing stock and has already made a mark for himself in motorsport circles.

By Dale Smith
Sports Writer

NATIONAL I.K.F. CHAMPION 1989

OUR BABY

Name GREGORY WILLIAM

Born at ST. MARY'S HOSPITAL

On APRIL 22, 1975

Time 2:48 P.M.

Weight 7 lbs. 4 oz.

Parents RIC + DONNA MOORE

Plymouth

INTERNATIONAL I.K.F. KART FEDERATION

FOSTER BROS. Racing Engines
Piston Port Development

1

A STUNNING DEBUT

The athlete who bursts upon the scene has taken a huge step at a young age towards a star quality others never will achieve over long careers. When the breakthrough is unexpected, the impact is heightened. Greg Moore opened more eyes, wherever knowledgeable racing eyes were watching, by finishing seventh in his first major league race than he might have by winning.

Celebrity always rested easily on his shoulders. Autographs, media interviews, photo ops — "Just one more, please?" — Greg Moore accepted it all as part of the game, and never stopped smiling.

He looked like a kid on the way to the library. Who'd have figured he was on the fast track to the top of the world.

It was not *that* he finished seventh, but *how* he finished seventh. He did it with spirit and flair. He did it with bravery and youthful exuberance. But mostly he did it with preternatural skill: an ability to run wide where others dared not. The passes the 20-year-old executed that day in Florida turned heads. Then those same heads nodded knowingly. Greg Moore was the real thing.

Had he won his debut Championship Auto Racing Teams (CART) race at Homestead Motorsports Complex, south of Miami, in March of 1996, experts might have judged that the bulk of the credit was due to a superior team preparing a superior car.

Had he won, Greg would have been applauded for his aplomb and maturity, but that would have been tempered by the common wisdom that victory on a banked oval can have as much to do with engineering as driving.

What rendered Greg's seventh-place finish remarkable was that, in its execution, he passed the eventual winner. Climbing back after a penalty had dropped him a lap behind the leaders — a full mile and a half on the Homestead oval — Moore darted by every car in front. Some drivers were startled to see the blue-and-white car jump up in their mirrors. It was to be veteran Jimmy Vasser's first career victory, but his sweet memory of his checkered flag is shared with another memory — of the image in his mirror.

Pre-race thoughts before the start of the inaugural U.S. 500 in Michigan in 1996 for the Vanderbilt Cup, replica of one of the sport's oldest trophies, put up in 1904 by railroad magnate William K. Vanderbilt.

"I said into my radio, 'What the hell?' when I saw this blue car coming behind me," Vasser recalls. "They came on and said, 'It's okay. It's Greg Moore. He's one lap down.'"

At the finish line, the kid from Maple Ridge, British Columbia, trailed first-place Vasser by only 20.660 seconds, as he closed fast on sixth. The feeling among those who were there that day was that Greg Moore did not get beat, he just ran out of laps.

Vasser, who became a close friend of Greg's despite more than a decade's difference in age, would never forget that outside pass. And he was not the only one who knew they had seen a champion in the making.

Far away from Homestead, Norbert Haug, the head of Mercedes-Benz Motor Sports Group, fabricators of the engine powering Greg's Reynard chassis, was watching on television with Dario Franchitti, then a Mercedes touring car racer, in a paddock at a race track in Europe.

"Norbert saw right away that Greg was something special," Franchitti said. "He became a huge fan — and from that point on, Greg was considered part of the Mercedes family."

The headline in *The Miami Herald* the next day captured the accomplishment. "Moore comes to pass . . . and pass . . . and pass."

The Herald story reveals that Greg knew

When the starting flag drops, friendships fall with it. Buddies Jimmy Vasser, Alex Zanardi, and Moore qualified 1-2-3 at the Michigan Marlboro 500, but only Vasser, who placed ninth, was around at the finish.

The Lights fading in the distance, Greg – here with Player's development team cohorts (l to r) Claude Bourbonnais, David Empringham and Bertram Godin – relished a new set of challenges when he stepped up to CART.

Moore moved his $1 million car onto the track at Long Beach — clean, sleek and 47 laps from the repair shop.

what he had accomplished, but, more important, that he knew what he could have accomplished. He told reporters he could have won the race, but for his own error. His car had been capable of winning. He had made a rookie mistake by passing the turtle-paced car of Juan Manuel Fangio II after the amber lights had signaled a caution period.

Greg downplayed his spectacular comeback. "In a situation like that you put your head down and go for it," he told reporters. The phrase, "put your head down," was to become a Greg Moore trademark response.

The thinking mirrored his father's. Ric Moore was in his son's pit in Homestead, as he was in the pit wherever Greg raced. As they hugged after Greg stepped out of his Player's/Forsythe Reynard Mercedes, there was no need for Ric to remind Greg to say the right thing. It had all been ingrained years earlier.

"I used to tell Greg, 'God gave you two ears and one mouth, and they need to be used in proportion,'" Ric remembers. Another thing the father told his son: Don't whine. Still another: Never blame the car.

The senior Moore, often described by his son as his father, manager and best friend, had been a racer himself in the 1970s, building his own car in which he competed in club events at Westwood Motorsports Park near Vancouver, British Columbia. On occasion, he had raced in the fabulous Can-Am series when it visited Edmonton, Alberta. There, he shared the track with the likes of Formula One world champion Bruce McLaren.

"I really wasn't very good," Ric says. "I just loved to go fast — and in those days Group Seven cars went more than 200 miles per hour. We didn't know any better."

Whether his own accomplishments were limited by talent or by equipment, Ric Moore was a mentor-in-waiting. By the time Greg was 10, he was his father's dedicated student.

"Once you get in your car, you cannot control what your car is, you can only do your absolute best with it," was one of Ric's familiar homilies that Greg surely remembered that day at Homestead.

"It may be a car that is a 10 out of 10, it may be a car that's a six out of 10. Maybe the engine is not working right, or the chassis, or you've missed the aerodynamics package," Ric elaborates. "Your job is still the same. If you are a 10

"I remember his first race at Homestead. I fell out of the race early and he was coming through the field and making outside passes and I remember thinking this guy is crazy! But he was making these outside passes work and it was unbelievable to see. That was my first memory of him as a competitor. I thought, Man, this guy is going to be tough once he gets it all figured out." **Paul Tracy**

"In 1996, when I was doing Indy Lights, I knew this guy Greg Moore had won 10 races out of 12, and everyone said, 'This guy is very good.' I watched his first race at Homestead and it was fantastic. So I said, 'Jesus, this guy is very good.'" **Tony Kanaan**

every day regardless of the car, then you've done the absolute best you can do."

Greg knew that Steve Challis, the race engineer from North Vancouver who had climbed through the ranks with him, had belted him into a car that was a 10 that day at Homestead. And so he waited for a quiet moment in the garage, after all of the interviews were over. Then he apologized to his father and he apologized to Pieter Baljet, the family friend he had come to consider a big brother. Greg said his mistake had kept them from winning.

"He blamed himself 100 percent. I'm not an emotional person, but I cried at the end of that race," Baljet recalls, "because you only get one shot at winning your first race and Greg should have won that race.

"We were all disappointed, but we left Homestead with great optimism. We all saw that weekend what was in the cards for Greg."

The confidence was justified. At the next CART race, held outside Rio de Janeiro, Brazil, Greg came within 18 laps of his first win — leading twice but dropping out with motor failure just after brushing the wall. Two weeks later came his first podium as Greg, three weeks short of his 21st birthday, finished third in the streets of Surfers Paradise, Australia, behind the veterans Vasser and Scott Pruett.

In his first CART season Greg experienced

"He can tell what I'm thinking by the look on my face," Moore said of chief mechanic and friend Steve Challis, an understanding so subtle, said Challis, "it's almost like a second language. We really don't dwell on the winning. That's the long-range goal."

two of the givens of big-time auto racing. One is that fun is never far away. After Greg tangled with Brazilian driver Christian Fittipaldi at Long Beach, California, putting them both out of the race, Fittipaldi made a show of threatening the rookie as they stepped out of their bent cars. Later that night, Greg found a life-sized cardboard figure of the Brazilian tucked into his hotel bed. Members of his crew had slipped the promotional figure into the room as a prank.

A second given is that there is inherent risk. All laughter within the CART community ended abruptly in mid-July of 1996 in the wake of the deaths of driver Jeff Krosnoff, track marshal Gary Avrin and a spectator in a crash during Toronto's Molson Indy. Krosnoff went airborne after touching wheels with another car, then struck a post. The driver died of massive head injuries.

Greg had liked Krosnoff and he was devastated. He had driven by the remains of the car in the aftermath of the accident. "How much he saw, I don't know," Ric says. Ric and Greg had a sit-down talk afterward. "I said to Greg, 'It's part of this job. People die. That's the way it is.'"

Perhaps Ric was remembering a friend, Stan Burnett, who had died in a Group Seven car that Ric had intended buying and racing two decades earlier. After Burnett's death, the senior Moore harbored no illusions about the risks in motor

Previous pages: Into the hairpin at Laguna Seca. "If you give any thought to crashing, you're not doing your job, you're not being professional," Moore said. "My biggest fear isn't crashing. My biggest fear is failure."

Throughout his career Greg was known as one of the cleanest drivers on the circuit. Incidents like this were few and far between. But when it did happen Christian Fittipaldi was involved more than once. It was more shove than punch, but Fittipaldi's reaction to the collision with Moore on turn seven in the Toyota Grand Prix of Long Beach

*The race driver's answer to the matador's
"suit of lights," the race day uniform
leaves no doubt about who's sponsoring
the car and the man inside. But the thrill
of putting it on never grows old.*

racing. He made sure his son understood.

"Still," Ric reflects, "I think when you're really good, you don't think of it happening to you."

Greg himself seemed charmed behind the wheel, even as trouble in the engine bay left him winless. In the U.S. 500 at Michigan International Speedway, for instance, he steered out of a frightening spin across the infield to stay among the front-runners and was in second place when he lost power.

Like his father before him, Greg relished the speed. He said, "Racing wheel-to-wheel at over 200 miles per hour, for me, that's extremely, extremely exciting." And the two-mile Michigan superspeedway offered higher velocities than any-where else on the CART circuit — at least until Roger Penske opened its western twin, California Speedway at Fontana, California, in 1997.

In that year's second race held at Michigan International, Greg was back on the gas again, qualifying third, one position ahead of the more experienced Al Unser, Jr., averaging 233.501 miles per hour. Again, he led the race, only to fall victim to equipment failure.

The fledgling Player's/Forsythe team sensed victory was at hand, and so did Greg. Yet, when the 16-race 1996 schedule ended, Greg still did not have a win. He finished a creditable ninth overall in the driver's championship, and second in Rookie-of-the-Year points to Alex Zanardi, a Formula One veteran driving for CART's top team of the late '90s, Target/Chip Ganassi Racing.

Still, everyone recognized what might have been for Greg Moore. In that sense the season stood as a triumph. The family returned to Maple Ridge, with father and son hungry to get ready for the season to come.

Crowds and cars in full roar, logo-covered suits, and the adrenaline rush of flying around the tracks of the world at full bore. For Greg Moore, here with (l to r) Adrian Fernandez, Scott Pruett and Robbie Gordon, they were the breath of life.

The world

At racing speed it's never about you and the car, because you're no longer separate. From the moment you settle in behind the wheel the two of you are one, a single being alone in the blur of the chase. And there is no feeling to match it.

flys by at

220 mph.

NEW KID ON THE BLOCK

When he got back to the garage after his first CART race, Greg Moore apologized to his crew for a mistake he felt had cost him a spot on the podium. Back at the track, people were still buzzing over what he'd done after he made it. "Staggering," said Player's VP Operations Neil Micklewright, of

Moore's debut in the Marlboro Grand Prix at Homestead, Florida. "He's a driver, the most aggressive young guy I've seen in a race car in a very long time."

"A figure to be reckoned with, absolutely," winner Jimmy Vasser called him. "A fantastic debut," said Gil de Ferran, who finished second. "He caught me easily. He was running very fast."

Heady praise for a guy who finished seventh. But it was the way he got there that had heads turning.

He'd been penalized a lap and dropped to 17th at lap 70 for passing

on a caution flag. To get back on the lead lap he had to pass everyone. He did that, and in doing it posted the fastest lap of the day, zipping over the course in 28.35 seconds while the PA announcer struggled for superlatives to match his performance.

Moore was having none of it. "We had the fastest car," he said glumly. "We were strong all day. The crew did a great job. For sure I'd have been on the podium if I hadn't made the mistake."

But rookies make mistakes. That's why they're called rookies.

And while Greg Moore fretted over what might have been, others were taking the broader view.

In CART spring training, against only the clock, he had been consistently among the top three to five prospects.

Now, on a rainy-day run cramped by six yellow flags and a red, he had shrugged off adversity and battled back to seventh place with a combination of nerve, style, talent and showmanship.

Moore had proven he could run with the big dogs. And there were 15 races to go.

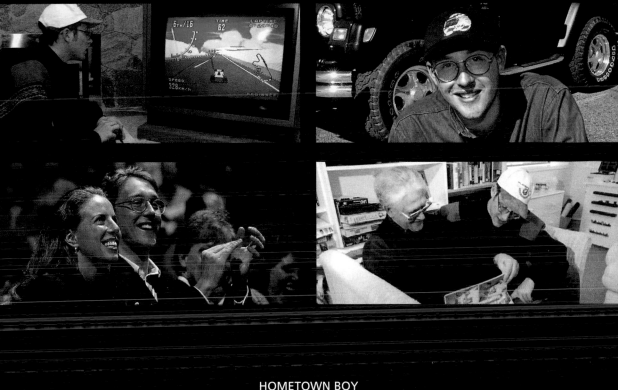

HOMETOWN BOY

He was reaching for the stars, but his universe pivoted around home. In Maple Ridge, British Columbia, population 62,000, he was just Greg Moore. "One night at dinner," Ric said, "we'd decided to cut back on gifts next Christmas because it had gotten crazy, presents piled ten feet around the tree."

Stepmother Donna Moore recalls, "Greg looked at James and Annie and then said 'Well, that may be okay for you adults, but not us kids.' He was 23 at the time."

Home was where he could join a wedding party for people he didn't know, jump up during the karaoke and burst into "Busta-Move". "He knew all the words, never looked at the monitor," says his friend Clint Van Blanken, who was spinning the music. "So he stays to the end of the party, then says 'Okay, I'm paying for the taxis home.' He knew few people there,

but he was making sure everyone got home safely!"

Home was where he and best friend Al Robbie would wind up at a pool hall, laughing and competing as if it was the final lap at Homestead. The last game's winner was officially declared "Emperor of the Universe."

Home was where he was forever poking his head around corners and screaming "Booo!" at Estella Bekessey, the long-suffering housekeeper who loved her "Gregorio" and gave as good as she got.

Once she asked for several

autographed pictures. "Stella, are you selling these?" he teased.

"Who do you think you are?" she sniffed. "Michael Jackson?"

Home was where five-year-old neighbor Matt Hayes knocked on the door in 1993 to give the famous big kid who lived there a good-luck drawing before a race. He did it every race thereafter. "He'd meet me at the door and say, 'Hi, Matt, how you doing?'" Matt remembers. "Every day I could talk to him. At school, when we talked about news, I'd talk about what position he was in. He was my friend."

Fame was great, but home was better — whether kicking back playing the CART video game, tooling around in his jeep, relaxing with dad, or taking in a Grizzlies basketball game with friend Amber Hamilton.

RACING HIGHLIGHTS

The word appeared in the CART official yearbook to describe his recovery from a penalty in his debut race at Homestead, but it could easily have described his entire rookie season: "Astonishing". Critics said Greg Moore was too aggressive, that sometimes his enthusiasm ran amok. He collided with

Andre Ribeiro in Detroit and again in Mid-Ohio. He crashed at Long Beach after colliding with Christian Fittipaldi.

But no one disputed the unadulterated talent and drive of the rookie from Canada. The last Indy Lights season had given a hint that he might be someone special. Three trips to the podium in his first CART season — third at Surfers Paradise in Australia, second two weeks later at Nazareth, Pennsylvania, and third again at Cleveland — put truth to the rumor. It could have been even better.

Mechanical troubles did him in with 18 laps to go at Rio, where he twice held the lead, and again in both races at Michigan International Speedway. As the season progressed they watched him learn to temper his rookie enthusiasm and natural aggression with the patience to wait, to recognize and seize the moment when it came.

Racing legend Mario Andretti was impressed with how the young Canadian carried himself, on and off the track. "Watching Greg when he first came on the scene, I thought, 'What a sharp, articulate, intelligent

guy'. He was very professional and mature for his age. He always had something to say, but he didn't just ramble on. He said something meaningful. And of course his driving was the same. He was going to make a mark for himself, no question."

Rookie driver. Rookie race engineer. New equipment — and ninth place in the standings at season's end. Clearly, this wasn't just another kid up from the Indy Lights circuit taking his lumps and wondering if he had what it took to play with the big boys.

Around the circuit, they knew CART had a new fast gun.

"He was definitely one of the best guys I've ever seen driving a race car," says Gil de Ferran. Third at Cleveland (l), third at Surfers Paradise (c) and second at Nazareth (r), the rookie took CART by storm.

2

MAPLE RIDGE ROOTS

The event is a common one and a special one: Father and son going off together for that first memorable look at the son's first car. The object of desire may be beautiful only to the young beholder. For Ric and Greg Moore, that special day took place in 1981 when father took son to his auto dealership, Maple Ridge Chrysler, to see that first car. Greg Moore was six years old.

Toy cars and small boys vroom-vrooming their way around living room carpet borders that become race tracks, remote control models dodging through kitchen-chair obstacle courses — the racing bug bites early.

Snapshot memories: (Clockwise, above left) Greg at four, doing the doggie pillow trick with Babe and Ada; saying goodbye to Mom on first day of school; the young Santa Claus and assistant elves; school sports day, one year away from the day he'd take the wheel.

Over the years any auto dealer makes some out-of-the-ordinary trades and, undoubtedly, there have been trades that Ric has turned down. Still, he recalls having accepted as partial payment over the years a monkey, an electrical generator, a Doberman and, in this instance, a go-kart with a miniature van body. Greg took to it right away.

"We weren't open on Sundays at that time," Ric recalls. "Just for something to do I'd take Greg down to the car lot on Sunday afternoon, and he'd just drive around and around the buildings on the lot."

"I think I picked off every one of the drain pipes," Greg told a reporter, remembering his first days behind the wheel. "There's still one that's bent today. My dad left it—my first trophy."

Scott Steele, then a mechanic who worked with Ric, recalls, "Every Monday morning when I came in to work, the kart would be sitting in my stall all bent up. My first job every Monday became getting that kart ready for the next Sunday."

By then Ric and his first wife, Donna Moore, Greg's mother, had separated. But, as Donna puts it, they remained on amiable terms and shared parenting equally. Ric's commitment to being a full-time father never wavered. He was devoted to providing his son a foundation of love and ideas.

Ric's own childhood had left him wanting. His father had "disappeared," as he puts it.

What kind of a Father's Day gift does a six-year-old give a special dad who'd become your best friend in the whole world? What better than a hand-drawn card of the two of you, close together as always.

Promised visits were missed. His stepfather, Cliff Moore, was "a good guy," but Ric chose to leave home and begin his own life at the age of 16.

The atmosphere for Greg was dramatically different, and he chose to stay home to the point of it becoming a family joke. Even after he had signed a multi-million-dollar contract with Marlboro Team Penske in the summer of 1999, his road always led back to Maple Ridge.

Maybe that impulse had something to do with his father being his friend, manager and mentor. Certainly it had something to do with Greg's ease with Ric's second wife, also named Donna, and with his step-siblings James and Annie. With Greg as with Ric, family life was something considered precious, to be devoured joyfully.

Icons of Greg's childhood remain in his first home, where his mother still lives, in Coquitlam, another commuter-belt Vancouver suburb not far from Maple Ridge. The Big Wheel plastic tricycle, the front wheel worn to nothing from the boy's skids, sits in the basement along with his Star Wars figures. Greg's early attempts at carpentry remain near the Santa Claus suit his mother has kept since he was five.

The mother's memories are of a serious little boy, one who wanted a hug and a kiss every night before sleep. "Being an only child, we spoiled him rotten, but he knew he was spoiled and was a

Dear Dad I am sowhrery I popt the soccer ball. That you pade 10 dollers four it. I love you I kerd about it. Now I am sad. Now I no you are mad.

Sunday March 28/82

When a guy's "popt" a soccer ball, there's nothing to do but 'fess up. You can question the spelling, but there's no doubting the sentiment when seven-year-old Greg apologized to Dad. Note that the ball is dead-center in the net.

It was a meeting that defined love at first sight: Six-year-old Greg and the go-kart with the minivan body his dad had taken as a trade-in at the auto dealership where the star-in-waiting careened around the lot and into drainpipes

First Go-cart race at Westwood.

good kid," she explains. "Just like when he became a race driver, he never forgot how fortunate he was."

She, too, had been part of his earliest karting days after he'd advanced from lapping Maple Ridge Chrysler to lapping the Westwood track near the house in Coquitlam.

"The very first time, Ric couldn't get in the kart but I could, so I went out and was reasonably quick. Greg got in and decided he should go as fast as Mom. The next thing, all we could see was sawdust flying — he'd just tried going too fast around a corner."

Greg had decided at the age of 10 he wanted a real kart, not just the mini-van. It was on the way home from Riverside, California, where he'd watched his father and Pieter Baljet co-drive Baljet's racing Camaro in a six-hour IMSA Camel GT Enduro.

He'd asked his father to wave at him as he drove by in the race, Baljet remembers. That promise couldn't be granted for safety reasons, but Ric was more than willing when Greg asked for a real racing kart. "Why?" Ric asked, wondering what his son would reply. Greg said, with

characteristic determination, "I'd just like one."

There were two passions — karting and hockey — that ruled the seasons of Greg's preteen years, with racing not always dominating. Greg wanted to be a National Hockey League goaltender, his mother recalls, truly believing that some day he'd play for the Vancouver Canucks.

"One time he said to me, 'Don't tell anybody or people will think I'm weird, Mom, but I think I have a sixth sense when I'm playing hockey,'" she says. "He could somehow feel people around him."

"I asked him one time if he felt that in racing. He thought a minute and said, 'Yeah. I know where everybody is.'"

In goal he competed with grown-up intensity. Once when Pieter Baljet was standing behind the goal with Ric, one of Greg's struggling defensemen mishandled the puck and scored on his own net. "Greg threw down his gloves, screaming at the kid," said Baljet. "We just laughed. It was Peewee hockey, after all."

Greg's mother remembers another game in which Greg was shutting out the opposition shooters when his coach benched him to give the second goaltender time in net. "He was so upset.

"He's got God-given talent that's being nurtured. He's been winning all his life. When he was little and went to the track, six dads would walk over with stop watches because he was the target — the one every kid and every parent knew they'd have to beat. He already had that reputation. He's got the potential to be one of the best in the world." **Ric Moore**

The fame of the Maple Ridge kid with the 99 car spread as the trophies began to pile up.
(Clockwise, above left) Winning in Spokane at age 11; pouring it on in Portland; with Scott Steele (l)
and his dad; and racing through the rain in Tri-Cities, he became the dominant figure in go-karting.

Getting a shutout meant so much to him."

Racing a kart, on the other hand, involved no one else at all once you were out on the track. When racing, Greg came to realize, the driver soars or fails according to his own actions. The race driver engages in a solitary exploration of risk and consequence, a game all the more exhilarating as the other players shrink in your mirrors.

At age 13, Greg chose karting over hockey. "We were on the way back from a race at Spokane, Washington," Ric remembers, "having raced in the Nationals in New York State before that, and I told him I'd arranged a week at goaltending school.

"He said, 'Dad, I think I'd rather take the winter off and go on skiing and karting.' I think he'd got tired of hockey four nights a week, with all the hours shuttling back and forth between games and practices. So, it was his decision to give up hockey."

A misconception involves the No. 99 that graced Greg's cars from karting days forward. Sports fans saw it as a tribute to Wayne Gretzky, the hockey superstar, but Ric explains it as the luck of the draw. "If you wanted to race at Westwood you had to join the Westwood Kart Track. When we signed him up Greg was the 99th member."

And though Greg greatly admired Gretzky, his idol was Brazilian Ayrton Senna, the three-time

In the Moore family, balance never meant just keeping your car upright. The home rules were simple: If you want to go-kart, fine. But your grades stay up, your head stays the same size, and you stay out of trouble.

Formula One world champion. Senna towered above every driver of his day before he was tragically killed in an accident at the Grand Prix of San Marino in 1994. A Senna poster dominated Greg's bedroom wall. Senna books filled his shelves.

There was one more fling with hockey when a call to fill in for an injured goaltender brought him back to playing, briefly. A teammate that winter of 1988-89 was 14-year-old Paul Kariya. That was the final time Greg strapped on the pads. The path to glory that would lead him to Player's/Forsythe was set as surely as Kariya's was toward the National Hockey League and the Mighty Ducks of Anaheim.

Racing could not be merely an interest, Ric Moore told his son. It came with lots of requirements. "When he decided he wanted to compete on the kart racing tour with races in Washington, Oregon and B.C., we made a deal," Ric explains.

"We'd buy a new go-kart, but I told him he'd have to work at this thing. We weren't going to play around. The deal was, he had to maintain a certain grade point average at school, he had to be a good citizen with his mother and me and he had to stay out of trouble."

Ric Moore's standards were even tougher at the Westwood track. Once Greg, who was responsible for bringing his own gear, forgot his neck brace, which all karters wear to protect

Westwood Jr. Stock,
first place, 1986.

Greg winning the Gold Cup race in Portland, Oregon.

Portland, 1990 Grand
National Championship in
Kart-O-Rama, junior class.

The other pursuit: sponsorship. Greg with his trophies, part of a
promotional package in search of support.

A pennant from the U.S. Grand Prix West in Long Beach, shots from the go-kart days, championship karting jacket. The memento pile kept on growing.

themselves in rollovers. The Moores packed up and went home without starting.

"He'd slide the car around a corner and I'd call him in," Ric says. "I'd say, 'How did that feel? It felt great? Well, look at the stopwatch. It cost you two-tenths of a second, and if you do it another time, this day is over. We're going home.'"

Scott Steele, who tended to Greg's racing cars all the way to the first year of Indy Lights in 1993, remembers the father's coaching yielding immediate results.

"Greg was so receptive to ideas and had complete faith in his father," Steele explains, "and at the same time he had this sense. He could just feel the speed, so he was unbelievably consistent. You could set a spot on the track at a corner and he'd hit it 50 times in a row and never miss.

"I believe that's what made him so good at the CART level: the consistency. He might not always have had the car to be blindingly fast. But someone else would make a mistake that cost half

a second. So Greg would gain that half-second."

The constant rain at Westwood, where karts ran on slick tires regardless of the weather, also played a part in Greg's uncanny ability to find the "edge," the point of no return beyond which traction evaporates. Ric realized as much at Portland International Raceway where, in the rain, Greg won the 1989 North American Enduro Kart Racing Championship. He was 14 years old.

Greg spun in that race and fell half a lap back, then was cool enough to read the leader's gauges as he passed him to retake the lead. Ric Moore concluded that his son had a future in motor sports.

After Greg won the karting championship again in 1990, the Moores decided to order a Van Diemen Formula Ford racing car from England. Greg Moore's first step beyond karts would be Canada's major Formula Ford series. At the young age of 16, he would now race against veterans twice his age.

Joe Kool, shades and all, hanging out with his wheels. At 13, a confident Greg looked ahead to the time when he would climb behind the wheel of a real car — and get a driver's license.

Most of his

He knew the names of all the world's great drivers and dared to dream that one day he might be among them. Karting triumphs merely whetted his appetite. There were bigger tracks, bigger challenges, bigger worlds. One day, he would face them. It was almost time.

role models

were racers.

Facing page: For Ric Moore, here in his 1977 Group Seven Racer at Seattle International Raceway, driving was a passion shared.

GARAGE OF DREAMS

It was called Gasoline Alley — not the famous one at Indy or the one in the comic strip, just a small service station in North Vancouver, B.C., where Steve Challis could work on high-performance cars and dream of the day he'd work on the ones flying around the world's greatest tracks. It was here

that Greg Moore's first car was lovingly, painstakingly assembled.

It came in a box almost as big as the car itself. Suspension, tires and parts packed around the tube frame, a Formula Ford Moore would race in the Formula 1600 series. "Pretty easy, actually," Challis recalls. "Probably took a week to get everything just right."

He'd been a driver himself, competed against Ric Moore at Westwood, and later worked on his cars when Ric was driving IMSA and Trans-Am. Now he was working with the next generation, a bespectacled

16-year-old who didn't say much. Who knew he'd wind up being a sort of older brother-road roommate-friend as they rose through the ranks together.

From the beginning, it was Operation Shoestring, Challis getting the car ready, Moore going through the growing process. "In the beginning, he never thought he was doing anything wrong, it had to be the car," Challis says. "But he learned fast."

Kent Holden, who worked with Challis and shared space in Gasoline Alley during the Formula years, remembers the jump to Indy

Lights and the winter testing in Phoenix when noon break would come and the mechanics would keep working while Moore went out to pick up their lunch.

"That's how small our team was. The driver getting lunch? But Greg never minded, never played the hero driver, you know? The thing I remember most about him, and if you talk to any of the other mechanics you get the same thing, you never really thought of him as a driver. He was just one of the team like the rest of us, who just happened to be the guy who drove."

The gamble was taken, the money spent, and now the dream was beginning to take shape. As the Van Diemen Ford 1600 was assembled, 16-year-old Greg could sit in the cockpit and have it built around him.

Leading the pack in the Mont Tremblant Shootout, Quebec, 1991. "I watched him go around (at Mosport) and I thought, 'there's some competition for me'. There were guys who'd been doing Formula Ford for 15 years who weren't doing corner two like he was." **Two-time Canadian Formula Ford champion, Stephen Adams**

CROSSOVER DREAM

The goalie pads were put aside early, one dream forced aside by another. But Greg Moore, the driver, never lost the passion for hockey that fueled Greg Moore, the Peewee goalie, who had played briefly with a legend-in-waiting named Paul Kariya. Already a racing star in his own right, Greg was just

another fan in August of 1996, when Team Canada was training in Vancouver for the first World Cup, begging Vancouver Canucks General Manager Pat Quinn for an introduction to Wayne Gretzky.

"He was infatuated with hockey players and we were infatuated with his talent," says ex-Canuck Garry Valk, who first met Greg on the celebrity golf circuit. "He wanted to know everything about life in the NHL."

Kariya, the Mightiest Duck in Anaheim, recalls time spent with Greg at the 1998 All-Star game in

Vancouver, two young athletes who had made it in their chosen sport comparing experiences.

Brendan Morrison, once a minor hockey opponent of Greg's, became a good friend as their journeys to athletic stardom proceeded — Greg on the track, Brendan on the ice. In their high school yearbooks, their inscriptions to each other promised a Stanley Cup for Brendan, an Indy 500 victory for Greg.

"Basically, we just wanted to wish each other the best of luck. It was nice to have somebody to root

for," says Morrison, who was traded to the Canucks in March 2000. "I watched him race as much as I could."

When athlete meets athlete, particularly those from different sports, there is an initial watchfulness, a scouting report, if you will, to be passed along to others. Greg Moore, according to Valk, was first-class.

"He was above his years in maturity," Valk says. "At 20, he acted more like 30. He handled his success well. At golf tournaments, he'd make sure all the kids got autographs. He had nothing but time for those kids."

The path not taken: Had the racing bug not bitten early, Greg the goalie might have indulged the sport that briefly ran head-to-head with his kart.

RACING HIGHLIGHTS

In retrospect, karting over hockey was the logical decision. At 13, Greg had three years of karting
behind him and was already beginning to draw looks from racing people who saw something special
beginning to take shape. "I remember the first time I saw him drive," says Tony Morris, a veteran of

he Canadian racing circuit in the 1980s and '90s who, a few years ater, would let the 16-year-old Moore use his race car for a lap around the Westwood track in Coquitlam, British Columbia.

"It was at the Westwood go-kart track. My kid was running and Greg went out for the first time. I can't honestly remember if he won his first race, but he was definitely one competitive driver."

Definitely.

From the first time he sat in a kart, Greg was pushing the enve-ope, honing his driving skills to go

with an instinctive understanding of the line between traction and picking yourself up off the track. It was at this point that he began to develop what he later called his greatest driving asset — patience on the track — as contrasted to what he saw as his biggest flaw — impatience off it.

Hockey was still a major love, a team sport, and a great one. Driving was a team sport, too, in terms of car preparation and race planning. But behind the wheel, it was boy-on-boy, and Greg reveled in it.

And, as he'd promised his Dad, they went at it seriously, full bore.

At 14, he won the first of two straight North American Enduro Karting championships.

At age 15, he balanced school with commuting to Ontario to attend the Spenard David racing school, where he finished first. Spenard saw a natural talent, "an ability to push the car to the edge in a way you do not see with the average student."

At 16 — hey, at 16 you could drive real cars! And that would be a whole new game.

At 14, he was the veteran, the champ, the king of the go-karters. Fast track or wet track like
the Tri-Cities (above) he was automatically considered the kid to beat. Not many did.

3

A RAPID RISE

Scenes from a five-year apprenticeship. Think of them as snapshots from a family photo album that traces Greg Moore's rise. The scenes run from his Rookie-of-the-Year performance in the 1991 Esso Protec F1600 Series, through to the 1995 PPG-Firestone Indy Lights Championship, in which he won an unprecedented 10 of 12 starts.

Facing page: If the shoe fits... Greg wears his Dad's old racing suit. Above: Firestone Indy Lights championship, first place, New Hampshire, 1994.

The snapshots are taken at Mosport, Ontario, at Phoenix International Raceway, at Nazareth, Pennsylvania. They come from wherever racing took Greg Moore. Always, though, the scene returns to Maple Ridge, British Columbia, as Greg Moore always did.

In the spring of 1991, mechanic Scott Steele arrived at Mosport, the historic motor racing track an hour east of Toronto, hauling Greg's newly assembled Van Diemen Formula Ford in a white horse trailer.

"I think some of them laughed a bit at the way we looked, showing up without a proper trailer," Steele chuckles.

The Esso Protec series was the country's prime proving ground for up-and-coming drivers. Steve Challis, new to the Moore team as engineer, warned Ric Moore on their flight to Toronto not to expect too much too soon. Breaking into the top 10 would be an accomplishment.

But Greg qualified second and went on to finish second in the race. "I was quite surprised to qualify behind the kid," said veteran racer Chris Bye. "But I figured that, during the race, most karters make mistakes when you fill their mirrors lap after lap. So I did that for 15 or 20 laps. He never flinched.

"He was quick and he was smart. Most of all he was frustrating."

Remembering those days, friends back home

Tight quarters, yes, but even at home in the driveway, for a race-car driver, it's the best seat in the house.

in Maple Ridge remark on Greg's ability to keep his racing separate from the life they shared with him.

There were, in effect, two Greg Moores. Race Track Greg was mature beyond his years. Maple Ridge Greg was a joker, a prankster, a typical 16-year-old top to bottom.

"It was during our years at Meadowridge School, that Greg was known as the class clown," remembers long-time friend Tanya Embree. "He always had the correct answers — but a wisecrack came along with them. There was nothing he was not good at. In band class he was a great drummer. But he'd get himself into trouble when he followed the teacher's comments with a hit on the snare drum.

"He loved having fun. One time, we were sitting in Mrs. Moore's car waiting for her when he pushed in a Beach Boys tape and started bouncing and wiggling around. After a few moments, he turned to me. 'What, you don't know how to car dance?' From then on, whenever Greg and I went out, the car dance was a ritual."

Alan Robbie and Tyler Williams, long-time friends from Maple Ridge, offer a story of an exquisite telephone prank. "At Zu, the pool hall where we'd hang out, the owner, Dominic Merlo, is known to get angry if he's interrupted while making a key shot," explains Williams.

"This one night, the pool hall phone rings just

It was a long way to go to school, Maple Ridge to Ontario, but when it's the Spenard David Racing School, you're 15, your major is car racing, and you finished at the head of the class, who complains?

Formula Ford practice day at Westwood, B.C. for a 15-year-old Greg at the wheel.

*Triumphs achieved taste even better when they are triumphs shared. (Clockwise, above left)
With Mom; with brother James and Dad; with family friend Pieter Baljet at the Buck Baker
Driving School in North Carolina, all gave success a touch of home; then it was a uniform of a
different kind as he and Tina Dale were off to the grad ball in 1993.*

July 21, 1991. The Moore family expands and Greg now had James and Annie to love, tease, and torment. "He was a joker," James says. "He'd do things like wet his finger and stick it in my ear when I wasn't paying attention."

Greg and Annie, Okanagan Lake, 1994. "A lot of the time he'd do really nice things, take me to dinner or drive me to the SkyTrain station, give me twenty dollars, and say, 'Go get yourself something.' Cool things like that."

as Dominic is about to shoot. He answers. Nobody's there. Another shot, 'Ring, ring'. An angrier Dominic again finds nobody's there. This happens six or seven times in a row. Finally, he discovers it's Greg, on the other side of the room, calling on his cell phone. At the time, Dominic didn't see the humor in it."

Greg reserved his serious side for racing. In 1992, Roger Bailey, an Englishman who was running the Indy Lights series, got a call from Ric Moore requesting a meeting. Ric's 17-year-old son had won the USAC Formula 2000 West Championship that summer. They wanted to find a way for him to move into Lights in 1993, even though he'd be underage for the first two races. The Toyota/Atlantic series had already turned him down.

"We were in Vancouver as part of the Molson Indy, and we agreed to meet," Bailey remembers. "We meet, and I say, 'While we're waiting on Greg, let's go into this bar and have a drink.'

"Ric said, 'This is Greg.' I look, and here's this scrawny little kid wearing rimless glasses. He looked like he should be playing chess." But there was something about Greg's demeanor that persuaded Bailey to give him a chance.

"We were scared to death in that first race in Phoenix, because up to that point we'd never gone with anybody younger than 18," Bailey continues. "But he was on pace right away. The guy had tremendous car control and was very smooth, very fast."

Moore finished fifth. Bailey need not have fretted.

Another friend from his teen years, Tina Dale, came to know Greg Moore as the guy who kept coming to her drive-through window at the McDonald's where she worked while attending high school.

"In the beginning I didn't know he was racing, he kept it so separate from his life at home," she said. "I actually saw his picture in the paper — that's how I found out. When we started dating, he took me to some of his races.

"The first one was at Portland. He said he had to go for the drivers' autograph session, so I went over to see what it was like. There was a huge line for Greg. I was blown away. I'd had no idea.

"He said, 'No big deal: I'm a race car driver; you work at McDonald's.'" In his return to the

"When he was first with us, I didn't see Greg's humor. He was very serious. Very focused. Later as I knew him away from the track, I found out all about the humor. Behind the scenes during a promotion or a media tour, he was just crazy. And put him with Patrick Carpentier or Lee Bentham or Andrew Bordin, it was almost impossible for me to conduct a briefing, he was always doing jokes and asking questions that made no sense." **Francois Cartier**

Neck-and-neck at the head of the pack, Formula 1600, Shannonville, Ontario, 1991.

Greg's first Formula Ford 1600 race in 1991 brought him second place and a chance to share the podium with winner Stephen Adams (c) and third place Rick Bye (l).

Phoenix mile-oval in 1994, fully 18 and benefiting from his year's experience, he scored his first Lights win — from the pole, another first.

His mother was there. What she remembers most clearly was how well her teenaged son was handling his growing stature.

"He was driving me in a golf cart to my car, parked across from the track. When we'd got there and had said our goodbyes, some guys came up and said, 'Are you part of the shuttle service?'

"Greg said, 'Hop on, I'll give you a ride'. And until they asked him if this was his job, Greg never told them who he was. Only then did he say, 'No, I won the race that just finished.'"

Although Greg knew his father's finances were stretched in the summer of 1994 after a sponsorship for the family-owned team failed to come through, Ric kept the details to himself. But the dreams would end without money and something had to be done. Going into Phoenix, Ric in effect bet that Greg would win by paying $5,000 to a Belgian company that specialized in insuring such offbeat ventures as hole-in-one contests. "When Greg won we collected $20,000 prize money from Lights and another $15,000 from the insurance — $20,000 less the $5,000 I'd paid for the policy."

Still by mid-season, Ric found himself writing checks he could not cover. The blessing of friends

"It's not about the press. It's not about the notoriety or the celebrity status or anything like that. To me, it's all about driving the race car."
Greg Moore

came through. Prior to a race at Loudon, New Hampshire, long-time ally Darryl Issa, owner of Viper Auto Security, called Ric to ask how things were going.

"I said, 'It's tough, Darryl, we're winning but we have no money.'" The family home was mortgaged, all of Ric's properties were mortgaged, even the house that Donna, his second wife, had kept after their 1991 marriage was mortgaged to keep the race car rolling. Now there was nothing left to mortgage.

"Darryl said, 'Look, I've got $40,000 I can give you.' Then we went to Loudon and won, and we were able to finish out the year on winnings. Greg had known we were tight — but he never knew we were on the razor's edge."

While aiming for today, Team Moore always had its eyes on tomorrow. A meeting was set up with legendary CART team owner Roger Penske at the Nazareth, Pennsylvania, race as the Moores sought advice on Greg's career. Marlboro Team Penske already had a full house with drivers Al Unser, Jr., Emerson Fittipaldi and Paul Tracy. Still, Ric Moore knew about the value of contacts.

Father and son waited four hours outside Penske's office. As owner of the track as well as his team, Penske had a lot on his plate. "Greg said a couple of times, 'Let's go,'" Ric recalls. "I said, 'Son, this man is really busy — and what an

*USAC F-2000
Championship Series West,
Rookie of the Year, 1992.*

*USAC F-2000
Championship Series West,
Champion Driver, 1992.*

*First trip to the podium. Greg steers his Viper to a third-place
finish in Portland, 1993.*

*Toronto, 1994. Despite a broken brake rotar,
Greg held on to finish twelfth.*

First place, Firestone Indy Lights, 1994.

opportunity to get half an hour of his time.'"

What Ric hoped for, more than anything, was a commitment of backing for the coming 1995 season. When eventually they were brought inside, Penske wasn't prepared to offer backing, but they discussed such possibilities as Greg moving to Reading, Pennsylvania, where the Penske racing operation was headquartered, to attend college.

Next day, Greg Moore won the Indy Lights race. The payoff from the meeting with Penske was to come in October, when Greg was invited back to Nazareth to test a Penske Mercedes. For the occasion Ric bought him a red driver's suit, in Penske's sponsor Marlboro colors, barren of rival sponsorship crests. A nice touch.

Penske must have been impressed. Early in 1995, he asked for Greg to fill in for Al Unser, Jr., in a photo shoot at Firebird Raceway, near Phoenix, featuring the team's cars for the coming season.

"It was the first time I realized Roger might have some interest in me," Greg would recall.

By then he and his father had signed a five-year contract with Player's/Forsythe that would carry him through a final year of Indy Lights and, if he merited the progression, into CART.

Player's certainly hadn't planned to take on a second Lights driver. Claude Bourbonnais was in place for 1995, and it was understood that he would move up to CART in 1996. But Ric Moore was on the phone to Don Brown, who would later become chairman and chief executive officer of Imperial Tobacco Inc., makers of the Player's cigarette brand in North America. He dogged Tom Moser, the company's point man in motor sports.

In the end, Player's offered a contract. Winning 10 races out of 12 in that 1995 Indy Lights series, including five in a row, and scoring 242 points to win the championship by a 102-point margin, turned out to be more than merit enough for Greg to advance to CART. The stage was set for his 1996 debut at Homestead.

Victory in Cleveland clinched the 1995 Indy Lights championship.

Canada was home and Canadians yearned almost as much as he to see him win on home soil. But it was to happen only once, at the 1995 Indy Lights in Toronto. Greg, Ric and Stu Ballantyne savor the moment.

New challenges

"I look at all these young kids coming up walking around the pits with their briefcases and I think of Greg riding his BMX up and down the hills at Mosport. He was having fun, doing what he wanted to do. Greg never forgot why he was there. He was there to have fun." **Canadian driver Chris Bye**

couldn't arrive

fast enough.

JUST THE RIGHT MIX

"He didn't come across as shy," Jerry Forsythe remembers. "I had four teenagers myself; I can relate to them. He was just a lot younger than I'd anticipated. But he certainly convinced me that all he wanted to do was drive a race car." The leader of the Player's/Forsythe racing team was recalling his

first meeting with Ric and Greg Moore, the exploratory session to see whether he might be interested in signing and financing the next step up in the youngster's career.

"He talked about his interests to me, one of them being hockey. But racing seemed to be his love, and definitely what he wanted to do for the rest of his career."

Of itself, that wouldn't have been enough. Racing is swarming with kids convinced they're only a backer away from becoming the next Mario, the next Unser. Nor would the Moores jump to just any

team. The mix had to be just right.

Over the preceding two years, Forsythe had kept an eye on the Canadian youngster — watched him on the track, watched him working on his car and had watched his off-track demeanor.

"There was talent there," he says. "He just needed an opportunity to show what he could do. I assured his father we would give a real, first-class effort, the best possible equipment and crew, and that our goal was to put together a program that I felt would allow him to work up the ladder."

Within a few weeks, a deal was struck. It was fortuitous for Team Moore, which was running out of funds and in need of support to lift Greg's career to the next level. But it was fortuitous, as well, for Player's/Forsythe, as Moore ripped through that final, dazzling year of Indy Lights.

Beginning to end, the relationship was a great one.

"Over the years, I saw him develop both mentally and physically," Forsythe says. "It really hurts me to talk about it. I was so very proud..."

Finally, the big break — and just in time, too. When Jerry Forsythe signed the young Canadian to the Player's/Forsythe team, the Moores were down to their last dollar. Greg's thank you was to win ten of the season's twelve races.

RUNNING WITH THE BIG BOYS

You're 19. Michael Jordan calls and asks you to come shoot some hoops. Mark McGwire says come take batting practice. Wayne Gretzky invites you to play street hockey with him. Or, Roger Penske asks if you would like to come and test one of his cars. Roger Penske, whose team has

ust come off a 1-2-3 finish in the CART season and won the Indy 500. That Roger Penske.

An electronics test, not a speed test. A chicane in the straightaway to keep the speed down. But you're 19, you're just out of your second season in Indy Lights, and you're test driving the No. 31 car in which Al Unser Jr. had won the championship.

That was Greg Moore in 1994.

He and Steve Challis spent two or three days at the Penske shop, had a custom seat made for the car, then went to Nazareth, where

Moore became only the second driver (the first: Ayrton Senna) ever to drive a Penske car without being under contract.

Why?

"I really think that for Roger this was kind of a look-at session," says Ric Moore, "because they didn't have anything for him at the time. We'd been talking to Roger for some time. I think he was checking Greg out, seeing exactly what kind of a young man he was.

"It was an honor. We looked upon it as one of those steps we

hoped to take sooner or later, and it turned out to be sooner."

A few weeks later, Greg was called back to do additional testing in Phoenix. Al Nazareth he'd had Unser talking to and working with him. In Phoenix it was Rick Mears. For a young driver, how much better could it get?

Ric Moore has one other memory from that time.

"There was a bet at Nazareth that Greg would stall the car first time out of the pits," he recall with a grin. "It didn't happen Somebody owes us $5."

What better way to learn than to listen to the best? Greg, the Penske crew and Al Unser Jr.

"Back in 1990 and '91 we started hearing about this young up and coming driver who was winning in every series he got involved in. That was the first time I heard about Ric and Greg. I remember his first Indy Lights win. I was jumping up and down in the pit lane and it was hugs all around." **Rena Shanaman, CART**

RACING HIGHLIGHTS

He was roaring up the racing ladder so quickly: Formula Ford 1600 Rookie-of-the-Year and fourth overall with a win and two seconds in 1991; champion of the USAC Formula 2000 West with four wins in 1992; ninth overall with a third in his rookie Indy Lights season — it was easy

to forget he was so young.

He got his street driver's license three days after his 16th birthday and was on the podium after his first race five days later.

He flew to Detroit for a media luncheon and needed a ride from the airport because he was too young to rent a car.

But put him behind a wheel and he was old enough to turn the Indy Lights circuit into his personal playground. In his third and final year, he literally shot the Lights out. He won 10 of 12 races, including five in a row.

Greg might have swept the schedule in 1995, but for bizarre turns in the Detroit and Vancouver street races.

In Detroit, Greg qualified second behind Robbie Buhl. An extended caution period from just after the start left only a handful of laps of actual racing before the checkered flag fell. That was insufficient, with Detroit's notorious lack of passing possibilities, for Greg to overtake Buhl. Buhl won, with Moore finishing second.

In Vancouver, Greg started

from the pole and was clearly beyond the reach of every contender until Pedro Chaves bunted him aside coming off a caution period. He struggled to place fifth. By the post-race press conference, Greg had regained his sense of humor. Asked if Chaves was known for such tactics, he quipped, "He is in Vancouver."

Next race, a week later at Laguna Seca, California, Greg closed the year with a pole and a win.

And now the little team that could — and did — was ready for the next rung.

"He could have won them all. Ten firsts, one second, and a fifth.
He could have won them all." Kent Holden, mechanic and friend

4

CART'S YOUNGEST WINNER

Greg Moore became the youngest race winner in CART history on June 1, 1997. That was good but he wanted better — he wanted to be CART's youngest season champion. He was 22 years, 1 month, 10 days old that day at the Wisconsin state fairground.

First place, Detroit Grand Prix, 1997.

Milwaukee, 1997. Holding off a charge by Michael Andretti, Greg Moore (l) became the youngest driver ever to take a CART checkered flag. "You get to the point where you say, 'What do I have to do to win one of these things?' Then you get that first win and you think, 'Wow! That wasn't that hard!'" **Greg Moore**

Al Unser, Jr., had been 19 days older when he had first won at Portland in 1984. The recognition Greg received for his feat was welcome, but he had his eye on displacing Jacques Villeneuve, who had been 24 years old when he clinched the title in 1995.

Despite his youth, just over a year into his CART career, Greg seemed a veteran within the drivers' community. He had been a threat to win through most of 22 starts leading up to his breakthrough in The Milwaukee Mile's Miller 200. Anything seemed possible in the pale green of this budding summer. As with his classic debut at Homestead, Moore's position in the summaries at Milwaukee was secondary to how he got there.

He won with unmatched corner speeds — which compensated for lifting off the throttle on the straightaways to preserve fuel. In this way the Player's/Forsythe team was able to capitalize on a strategy of stopping only twice for methanol while others, including runner-up Michael Andretti, pitted three times.

The day was a triumph in terms of car setup for engineer Steve Challis. "We had a very good balance in the car," said Challis. "We were doing incredible lap times for the amount of gas we were using."

Above all, it was a triumph of Greg's maturing ability as a driver. The Milwaukee Mile, an

"The driver is the biggest variable. If the tires and engine and chassis are up to it, I think I can drive up there with the best of them."

Greg Moore

oval track noted for its lack of banking, is known to reward the driver who operates best at the limits of adhesion. Greg, having refined his craft on the slick Westwood kart track, found that to be second nature, maybe a sixth sense.

At 16, he had said, "It's like there are little fingers on the ground, just touching the tires. There's a feeling of being on the edge. For me, it's a neat feeling. It's exciting. For other people it might be scary because the car's at the edge of being out of control. If you're scared, you're not going 100 percent."

Now, six years later, that requisite fearlessness had brought him victory. "Racing with Michael [the acknowledged master of Milwaukee with five wins] and Jimmy [Vasser], for me it was one of my best drives," he said after the race. "I didn't get intimidated. I just put my head down and did my job."

That familiar comment — "Put my head down" — was classic Greg Moore. But one comment, overheard by only a few in the Milwaukee victory circle, would puzzle all but two of those present.

Fellow driver Max Papis, whose race had ended with his car crumpled against the wall, approached Greg, flashing a big grin, and uttered something about macaroni and cheese. It was a moment of connection between the two second-year drivers.

He attracted friends like nails to a magnet, breaking down the traditional competitive reserve. Greg and (left to right) crew member, Max Papis and Dario Franchitti — buddies until the flag dropped.

Car batteries aren't the only ones that need recharging. Away from the noise, the demands and the pressures that go with being a champion racer, Greg tries competition of a different sort: man vs. salmon.

*"He definitely was one of the best guys I've ever seen driving a race car.
He had such an ease with extreme situations."* **Gil de Ferran**

The night before, the two had been talking in Greg's motor home. Many of the CART drivers prefer these homes on wheels to hotel rooms week after week. It was Greg's vehicle that became the social center and Greg was the social focus among the paddock residents. Fun was always on the menu. Fine dining? Well, that's another story.

What Papis saw in Greg's place that night left him wondering about his friend's tastes and fearful about his native Italian cuisine. "About 9:30 in the evening Greg takes out a bag of macaroni and cheese, puts it in a pan, and I said, 'Hey kid, what are you doing?'" Papis relates.

"He said, 'Oh, I'm having my pasta.'" "I said, 'That's not pasta.'" "And he said, 'Oh, yeah, this is really good.'"

"I said, 'If you win tomorrow, I'm going to eat this stuff for the next three races.'"

"I went to the victory circle and he was cheering and I looked at him and said, 'Greg, macaroni and cheese!' And he looked at me and said, 'Macaroni and cheese, dude!' I remember the joy in his eyes. It was very special."

The Italian found himself consuming North American pasta-in-a-box for three races in which he finished 11th, 28th and 27th. It didn't work for him. Greg, though, went on to a second consecutive win, in the streets of Detroit's Belle Isle. He was blessed with good fortune when, in the last lap, PacWest teammates Mauricio Gugelmin and Mark Blundell ran out of fuel in front of him. The victory advanced him to third in the championship points race. Macaroni and cheese, indeed.

Greg's growing friendship with Papis, and with Dario Franchitti, was part of his metamorphosis from the bookish-looking boy whom Lights administrator Roger Bailey overlooked altogether, to the carefully groomed young man with a life of his own. He had become Greg Moore, individual, rather than Greg Moore, prodigy of Ric Moore and Steve Challis.

In those five years, two key life experiences contributed to his maturity. In one he discovered independence; in the other he began to see how highly the international racing community regarded his talents.

In the winter of 1994-95, prior to Greg's final year in Indy Lights, Ric had decided that Greg should get more real world experience by working

"We all recognized that he was someone who was eventually going to come to Formula One. I became aware of him when he raced Formula Ford 2000 cars. I saw him race and was aware of his upward progress. When he did so well straight-away in Indy cars, there was a lot of speculation about him coming to Formula One. He was very ambitious and committed to what he was doing. I saw him as a serious player and it would have been good for Ford and for our team." Jackie Stewart

*The sights, the sounds, the people — Greg Moore soaks up the life of a champion driver.
(Clockwise, above left) Signing posters, checking out the track and the crowd, just strolling
through the rain and a photo-op with boss Jerry Forsythe.*

with someone other than himself. Pieter Baljet agreed to put the 19-year-old to work at his Chevrolet dealership in Duncan, on Vancouver Island, a half-day and a ferryboat ride from Maple Ridge. Greg's first duty was telephoning service customers to ask if they were satisfied. He quickly advanced to service advisor.

"He had a knack with people," recalls Baljet. "He lived with me and in the evenings we'd watch tapes of Lights races. We'd study Bryan Herta and Andre Ribeiro for their strengths and weaknesses. He was a sponge for this stuff. I wasn't trying to tell him how to drive, though. The idea was to get him thinking, to make him a bit of a scholar of the sport, and that came naturally. We'd take a break, by the way, to watch "Beverly Hills 90210" with my eight-year-old step-daughter."

The second pivotal experience had come in June 1996, at the Canadian Grand Prix in Montreal. Although he had idolized the late Ayrton Senna, Moore had never attended a Formula One race. Now Mike Hurst, a long-time acquaintance of Ric and an advisor to Greg's management, arranged audiences with F-1 major domo Bernie Ecclestone and such team owners as Frank Williams, Eddie Jordan and Jackie Stewart.

"Bernie was very gracious and said he'd love to see him come to Formula One some day," said

Engine failure after 67 laps, Cleveland, 1997. What went wrong?

Hurst. "Everyone was aware of what Greg had achieved in his last year in Lights, as well as his performance in that first race at Homestead.

"That weekend I think opened Greg's eyes. At that stage his framework was pretty well Indy car racing. Now he understood that at some point he could enter that other world — Formula One."

The days of going unrecognized were behind him. In Lights days, he had once been refused access to the Milwaukee paddock. Despite being in his driver's uniform, and with helmet in hand, the security guard decided that he couldn't possibly be old enough to race. After his performance in the Miller 200, that sort of experience was over.

Being too young to rent a car, while old enough to race at 200-mph-plus, also had ceased being an issue. Throughout the early years he'd depended on the likes of Adam Saal, publicity director for Indy Lights, or Rena Shanaman, when she ran the Vancouver race, for rides to and from promotional appearances.

Whatever his fame or soaring self-confidence, some aspects of the Greg Moore persona remained unalterable. He remained a notorious prankster, a practical joker par excellence. And always he lived by the assumption cell phones had been invented so friends could talk any time, all the time, wherever in the world they might find themselves.

Previous pages: Pit stop pressure during a victory at Detroit. "It's not like a test session when you make a change and the guy can take a few laps to get up to speed. In a race he has to stand on it right away and trust your judgment. So the relationship is really important." Steve Challis

Miller 200 Milwaukee
Mile Champion,
first win, 1997.

Mid-Ohio CART world
series, second place, 1997.

Kicking back in the Grand Cayman Islands: sand, surf,
sunshine — and dreams of the season to come.

Well, it's not all work. Moore, Jimmy Vasser, and Richie Hearn at the
baseball tournament where Moore met, among others, Beverly Hills
90210 star Jason Priestley, who would become a close friend.

"My memory of Greg is his generosity. So often he paid for everyone. The Omega watches for fastest lap – every time he won, he gave the watch to friends and crew." **Francois Cartier**

Both humor and long-distance connections must have helped Greg remain positive, since his fortunes dwindled as the 1997 CART season wore on. Second in championship points going into the mid-season Toronto Molson Indy, Greg's standing tumbled as he failed to finish seven of the final eight races.

Characteristically, he put a positive spin on his misfortune. "At the beginning of the season I said, 'Every race I want to finish in the top five,'" he told a reporter in September. "Well, every race that we've finished, we have been in the top five. So, that way, it's going very well."

He stood ninth in points at year's end. The dream of surpassing Villeneuve would have to wait. In the final race of the year, at Roger Penske's new showpiece track at Fontana, California, Greg was in the lead with 10 laps to go when his engine shut down.

"Every time you have a bad result you kick it around on the way home," Ric recalls. "You'd give it a day because after the race there was too much emotion to talk about it.

"The thing you ask yourself is, 'Am a part of this, or am I the cause of this, or am I an innocent victim of this?'"

What Ric would remember with utmost clarity from 1997 would not be the extreme highs or lows that he believes are so exaggerated by the solitary nature of the sport. He talks instead of a letter he received some weeks after the Milwaukee triumph.

"A lady wrote a six-page letter telling me what my son had done that day, after winning the race. Her son, six years old, was suffering from leukemia, but in remission, and desperately wanted to go to the race.

"At the end of the day he was really tired, but when he and his mother sat down to rest, he spotted the drivers' motorbikes parked outside the winner's press conference. He rushed over, and when they came out, Greg sat down, lifted the kid on to his knee and spent five minutes with him. 'How you doing? Cool!'

"A couple of other drivers had ignored the kid when he had approached them. I'm proud my son always took time for kids, anytime he possibly could."

*"He had the ability to have a bad day, to make a mistake or have things go wrong around him that weren't his fault, and shake them off in a moment. He could put things behind him very rapidly." **Neil Micklewright***

Like a sunday

"He would wait for the car to be as good as we could get it and he would go out and do some of that Greg Moore stuff. Quite often he would bring performance or speeds out of the car that weren't inherently in the vehicle. And that was just pure Greg Moore." Neil Micklewright

drive, without

the picnic.

Driving for Mercedes at Laguna Seca, 1997. The Mercedes people found much to admire in the way the young Canadian was able to adjust to the demands of a different breed of car.

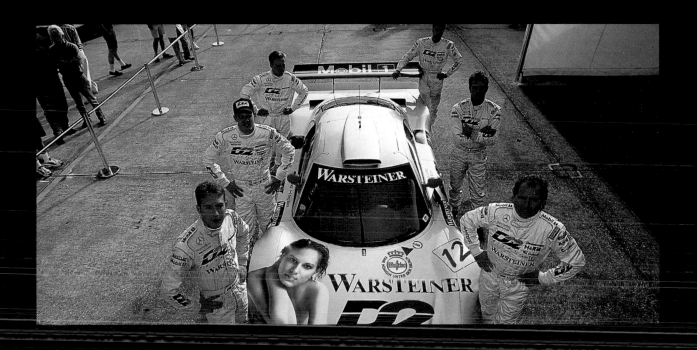

NEW STAR ON THE RESUMÉ

When the call came from Mercedes at the end of the 1997 CART season asking him if he'd like to join the Mercedes team for the final two races of FIA GT championship races in Sebring and Laguna Seca, Greg Moore's eyes lit up like Christmas. New car – a Mercedes CLK-GTR.

A new kind of driving. A chance to step, however briefly, into a new phase of the sport that would be his life. Who wouldn't?

"I didn't try to make an Indy car out of it," he explained. "I changed my driving style. I changed myself." That meant gentler breaking and shifting, and short, snappy movements of the steering wheel.

Originally scheduled to team with veteran Klaus Ludwig, who'd competed against Ric Moore in 1985-86, Moore wound up with

Alexander Wurz. They rolled through the rain at Sebring to finish an impressive seventh. At Laguna Seca, a podium spot seemed certain until a driver in a GT2 Porsche collided with Wurz who had been the fastest driver in training – while he was being lapped. The collision and resulting pit stop dropped them to eighth place.

Still, they had caught the eye of the Mercedes people, and when it was over, Moore had another star on his resumé.

"Moore is strong," said AMG team manager Hans-Jurgen Mattheis. "He offered up the best start in his new job that an AMG freshman has given us for ages."

Stars and Cars, the official Mercedes magazine, offered a post-season scouting report lauding the man as much as the driver.

"His demeanour is mostly serious. His answers are precise. His posture is so erect that he seems to be trying to get more out of his body than his 180 cm permit."

Moore, lower left, and the six-star three-car Mercedes squad for two American FIA GT championship races.

BEST OF FRIENDS

They had a deal, Greg Moore and his best friend, Al Robbie: If Greg's head started swelling, Al was to tell him, straight out. "It was in 1995 after he'd signed with Player's, and he'd just met someone who was stuck-up and snotty. So I said 'Fine. If it gets too big, I'll just punch you in the head.'"

It was that kind of friendship, born over Halloween fireworks when Robbie recognized him as one of the coaches at a kids' hockey game he had refereed the day before — the one who hadn't yelled even once, and came across the ice at the end to say "Good game."

Robbie was there, freezing in the snow, when the first Indy Lights car arrived and, naturally, they had to fire it right up while neighbors leaned out windows to find out what was making that infernal noise. A summer washing cars at the Moore auto dealership,

a help-out stint in a race at Portland — the first he'd ever seen outside of Vancouver — and suddenly there was Ric Moore, asking him to join the pit crew. Greg liked having him there, Ric explained. Said it relaxed him.

He was 18, just old enough to be in the pits. "Sign me up," Al said, and off they went to Laguna Seca. At Laguna, they ran timed laps — in the dealership's minivan. Robbie recalls almost flipping it. As fast as he went, Greg would smoke him.

The Moores got cell phones. In the first three months, Greg

logged 48 hours. Once Robbie had 19 calls in three days — all from Greg, all from Europe. Important stuff like "I just got to Finland. It's 6 a.m. God, it's cold!"

Strapped in the car on that last Saturday in Fontana, Moore radioed the crew, who turned, looked at Robbie and burst out laughing. "I was wearing shorts," he said, "and Greg had said 'Look at him! There's a set of legs any chicken would be proud of.'

"Just about to do his laps and he's cracking jokes," says Al Robbie. "That was him."

The Inseparables: Greg and longtime pal Al Robbie.

RACING HIGHLIGHTS

Greg Moore's second CART season was pure roller coaster. On one hand, he became the youngest driver ever to win a CART race and followed it a week later with a win in Detroit. Twice — at Surfers Paradise and in Rio de Janeiro — he'd finished second. Racing

luck, the kind he'd enjoyed in his dazzling final Indy Lights season, seemed to be with him. In Detroit, the two cars running ahead of him both ran out of fuel in the final lap. Eight races in, he was on a roll.

But in the final eight races, he finished only once, a second at Mid-Ohio.

Three times, he had engine failure. In Toronto, his car was clipped and sent into the outside wall by Alex Zanardi. At Road America, he slid off the rain-soaked course. In Vancouver, where he so desperately wanted to

win, he was out after 63 laps. In the latter two races, he knew where the fault lay. He saw his villain every day in the mirror.

And yet, there were grounds for optimism. He had come into the season with a plan: If he could stay in the top five each time out, he would be in contention for the prize that went beyond mere money – the PPG Cup points title. It hadn't worked out that way. But, for all his problems, he finished seventh overall in the season-end standings.

By the end of his second year,

he was now deemed a veteran in the community of drivers. He had made friends and settled in. Others continued to anticipate the Greg Moore who was yet to come.

Editors of the CART yearbook, picking their own Top 10 drivers for the season, boosted him to fourth. "Among his many attributes," they said, "are a refreshing honesty, a maturity beyond his 22 years, and Job-like patience."

He had, they conceded, made mistakes at both Road America and Vancouver. "But," they concluded, "his time will surely come."

More rain on the Moore parade. Electrical failure epitomized the latter half of the '97 season.

5

A WORLD OF POSSIBILITIES

Ric Moore was bedridden in Maple Ridge with pneumonia the weekend Greg
won his first pole, in qualifying for the 1998 Marlboro Grand Prix of Miami. He
was the youngest pole-winner in CART history. Pieter Baljet was able to provide
a play-by-play of Greg's 217.541 miles per hour lap by cell phone from trackside.
He handed the phone to the jubilant son as he stepped from his Reynard Mercedes.

Grand Prix of Brazil champion, 1998.

"You want to prove that you're not a flash in the pan here. You want to establish yourself." **Greg Moore**

"Dad, we did it," Greg was heard to say. "Thanks dad, thanks dad, thanks dad."

Reporters wanted to know the other side of the conversation. Greg told them his father's first words had been, "'Does this mean I can't come to any more races?' And I think there was probably a tear in his eye." With tears in his own eyes, Greg explained that his father hadn't missed one of his son's races in 13 years.

Second to Michael Andretti in the Miami race itself, Greg assumed the championship lead three races later with a third at Nazareth. He followed with a sensational win at Rio de Janeiro. Greg was on a roll.

The winning pass at Rio saw him soar by Alex Zanardi, reigning CART champion and master of the calculated gamble. Throwing a feint inside, Greg followed with an outside move that seemed to simultaneously harness centrifugal force and extend traction beyond reason. "I pulled a Zanardi on Zanardi," Moore told a close friend.

Mike Hurst was awakened early the next morning. "At six o'clock the phone rang. (Formula One team owner) Frank Williams was calling," recalls Hurst. "Frank said, 'That was a magnificent move your young man made in Brazil. What did you say are the terms of his contract?'"

Told Greg was under contract to Player's/Forsythe through 1999, Williams asked

"I'm just living my life as I go. I never think 'I don't want to be here'. I love every minute of it." Greg winning the US 500, Michigan, 1998.

to be kept up to date. Two more poles followed over the next three races, including Greg's first on a street circuit. But as June led into July, the season soured. Only a sensational win at Michigan, when Greg jumped past Jimmy Vasser in the final lap – the last of 62 lead changes made throughout the race – could have continued to fire Frank Williams's imagination.

Second to Zanardi in championship points after eight races, Greg failed to finish seven of the final 11. Frustrated by mechanical difficulties that made his car uncompetitive, he started taking chances. He spun at Houston after starting on the pole. He was leading at the Mid-Ohio road circuit when he hit Andre Ribeiro's car in the pits and was dunned a $5,000 fine for dangerous driving.

At Portland, Oregon, straining to overcome a 14th-place starting position, he tried to sneak up the inside to move to the front. Hitting a curb he became airborne briefly, then made contact, eliminating himself and two other drivers. After the race the chief steward placed Greg on probation.

"'Roger, that was one of the dumbest things I've ever done,'" Roger Penske remembers Greg telling him in the aftermath. Talking the next day, Ric Moore said to his son, "What I want to know is, who was that in your car? That wasn't Greg Moore."

His stepmother witnessed his struggle following

Pit stop, Homestead, 1998. Where a second's delay can cost a driver a trip to the podium.

Mission accomplished. Moore races back into battle and the crew can relax — until next time.

*Champagne for three: Runner-up Alex Zanardi (l), winner Jimmy Vasser, and
third-place Moore pop their corks after the 1998 race at Nazareth.*

every reversal. Always he'd come home to Maple Ridge — to his solitary fly-fishing at nearby Mike Lake, to hanging out in the company of his constant friends — but the strain was starting to show.

"I think it was frustration," she says, "and I think there may have been a kind of embarrassment that all of his peers were doing so well. Greg wasn't a whiner, but he was low toward the end of '98, like he was low late in '99. But you know what? He would not carry his frustration into the next race. The next race was always a brand new possibility."

His peers, primarily, meant Dario Franchitti, the Scotsman who by then was a close friend. Indeed, Franchitti's first CART win, at Road America, the fabulous rolling road circuit at Elkhart Lake, Wisconsin, in August of 1998, prompted the wildest celebration in Greg's racing career.

"When Greg scored his first win I was happy for him, but I didn't know him that well," recalls Franchitti. "With my win, well, I remember us waking up on a lawn at Siebken's (the venerable hotel favored by racers over the decades). It was like, 'How did we get here?' A great time!"

Ric Moore knew his son seldom drank during racing season. Greg was the perfect spokesperson for the Molson Breweries 'Take Care' program encouraging responsible drinking. "I heard about that night," says Ric. "I didn't really want to know the details."

He also was concerned, initially at least, about the friendship burgeoning among Greg, Franchitti, Max Papis, Tony Kanaan and Jimmy Vasser. "When we all started to become friends," says Franchitti, "Greg and I in particular, Ric was always saying to him, 'Be careful about getting too close. These guys are your competitors.'"

"He need not have worried about Greg. The Fontana race came only four or five days after Greg and I had shared an incredible motorcycle ride from Los Angeles to Laguna Seca. But I tried to pass Greg in practice and he came right down across the front of my car. Right then, it was clear the relationship was different when we were racing. I remember on the superspeedways we always waved any time we passed each other!"

Papis, too, wondered about growing close. From his racing in Europe, he was accustomed to tension among competing drivers. "In the beginning

"Most people knew Greg as a great driver. To me, Greg was a great friend. I looked forward to the times we could get together. Shopping, having a coffee, starting the occasional food fight at various dinners and on charter flights – but denying it. Hanging out in the F1 garages. It's all the little things that are valuable to me. This is how I remember my friend." Lee Bentham

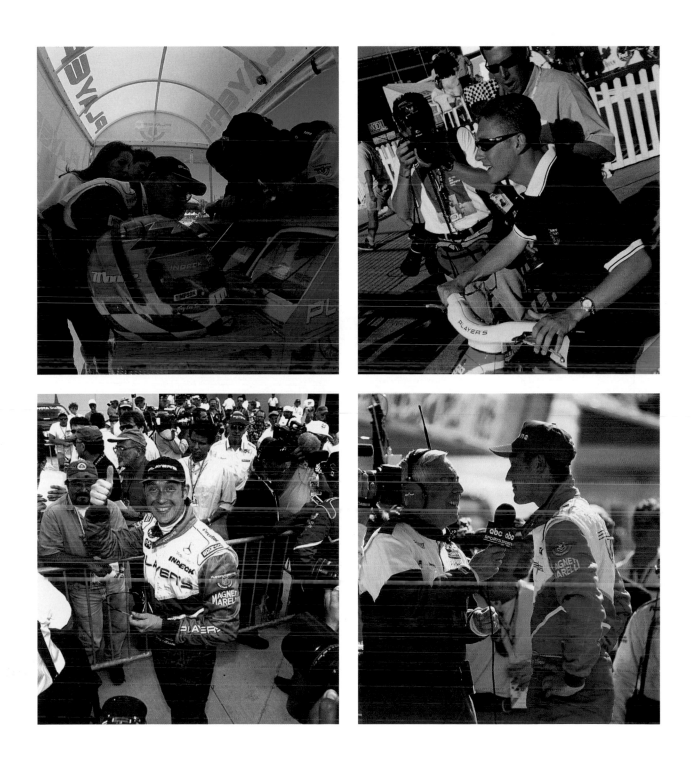

Clockwise, above left: Whether it was checking the latest telemetry; taking the scooter out for a spin; stopping for an interview or greeting the mob at Victory Circle, the pace was ever-hectic.

Surfers Paradise, 1998: Greg, Max Papis (l) and Dario Franchitti (r)
enjoyed some off-day surf time on the beaches of Australia.

Ever ready to try something new, Max Papis and Moore rig up for bungee-jumping at Surfers Paradise.

Drivers day on the beach at Surfers. "We all know how proud Greg was to be a Canadian, but I know that if he had to pick a second choice he would call Australia home." Rosko Dickinson, organizer Miss Indy Pageant.

I said to myself I had to be a little bit careful because is he going to be your friend for real, or not?

"But later on, the barrier went down because I realized, thanks to Greg and some of the other drivers, that here in America you are not obliged to hate your opposition. You can smile and hang out and have respect for them, and still go out on the track and fight them very hard — harder than anyone."

Friendships hadn't always been the rule among drivers. During the 1980s and through most of the '90s, drivers went their own way. "We used to have a lot more fun before we all started carrying briefcases," veteran driver Bobby Rahal remarks, fondly remembering the days of the Can-Am series in the '70s, when every race meeting ended with a communal barbecue.

The younger Moore was credited with helping bring back the fun. The trend toward drivers staying at the track in motor homes made it easier to get together, and the convergence of several fun-loving bachelors made it certain that there would be a good time. Greg was usually the organizer. "Hey, dudes, what's on?" was his signature greeting when he and his fellow 'brat pack' drivers gathered. One limitation applied. Moore was not about to move to Miami or Las Vegas, two places favored by CART's international cast. Life in Maple Ridge continued, no matter what.

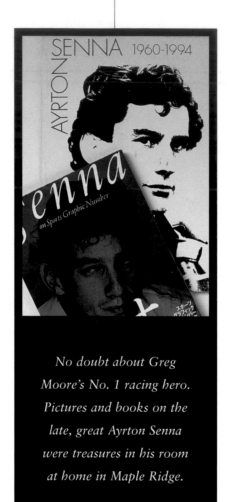

No doubt about Greg Moore's No. 1 racing hero. Pictures and books on the late, great Ayrton Senna were treasures in his room at home in Maple Ridge.

Following another Franchitti win, at Houston later in the '98 season, the friends flew directly to Australia for the race at Surfers Paradise. As a birthday present, Greg had buddy Alan Robbie flown in from Vancouver. Robbie found himself judging the race beauty pageant.

Franchitti, aboard the car that was the standard of the season, the Reynard Honda, won the pole and was runner-up in the race. Greg finished eighth, in the points for the first time since winning at Michigan. Australia that year would be remembered for good times with good friends.

The season finale, at California Speedway, always holds promise. In 1998, the result at Fontana typified the split nature of Greg's season. In the lead going into the final lap, he was victimized by Jimmy Vasser, who drafted by with ease. Greg had no time to launch a counterattack before the checkered flag fell. Greg understood; he'd beaten Vasser at Michigan under exactly the same set of circumstances.

Second on the podium was not ideal. But it was a reminder of how strongly the combination of Greg Moore and the Reynard Mercedes ran on CART's oval circuits. It was clear to everyone on the Player's/Forsythe team that they could only contend for the 1999 championship if they somehow found a way to be as competitive on road and street circuits as they'd always been on ovals.

Second place, Marlboro 500, 1998.

Moore takes his turn in the 1998 driver introductions at Homestead.

"I've had many kids drive for me. I brought Rick Mears off a back hoe into a car and Little Al and Bobby Unser Jr. and Pete Halsmer. I felt from the get-go that Greg had a lot of potential." **Bill Simpson, Simpson Safety Equipment**

A long way from Gasoline Alley: Greg, Steve Challis and Ric Moore share a relaxed moment on the CART circuit.

In racing season, you grab your relaxation when you can, whether it be golf,
pool with friend Tyler Williams, or just a good long run on the bike.

"That guy had more talent in his pinky finger than most guys in this room." **Paul Tracy, November 1, 1999, CART banquet**

Above: The broken steering wheel, a result of the incident at Motegi, Japan. Facing page: A Thursday crash due to a gear shift broken during practise in Motegi, Japan didn't stop Greg from finishing fourth in his backup car in Saturday's race.

But '99 was some months away. First Greg needed a break. The wedding of Jason Priestley, the fellow Vancouverite who starred in *Beverly Hills 90210*, was one significant diversion. Greg and Jason had become friends after playing on opposing teams in a celebrity softball game at the '97 Homestead. At Priestley's wedding, Dario Franchitti met actress Ashley Judd, which would ultimately lead to Dario and Greg spending far less time together in 1999.

The journey of discovery in Greg's life continued. He and Franchitti were invited to visit Papis at the Italian's family home at Como, in northern Italy. By day they karted, or toured Monza, the fabled Italian Grand Prix circuit, or shopped. By night they hung out together. And when they were done they flew to Helsinki, where F-1 world champion Mika Hakkinen had organized a karting tournament.

The highlight, undoubtedly, was where Greg slept at the Papis's. "When I was a kid I was a very good friend with Ayrton (Senna)," Papis explains. "Ayrton was Greg's hero, but he never met him. And I had Ayrton's helmet in my room, signed by Ayrton.

"Ayrton used to stay at my place all the time when he was coming to Europe, because my mechanic in go-karts was Ayrton's mechanic as well. There is a little guest room with two beds where Ayrton always lived when he was racing karts. I had always talked about this with Greg. So when he came to Como he was very excited and said, 'Hey Max, which one did Ayrton sleep in? Okay, I'm going to sleep in that bed. Dario can sleep in the other one.'

"Greg liked that a lot, and he was very proud."

Every race

was a new

possibility.

FOUR OF A KIND

Tony Kanaan recalls the good times when he, Max Papis, Dario Franchitti, and Greg Moore were the Brat Pack, and the racetracks, parties and friendships stretched over the horizon to forever. "He was my best friend," he says. "He's still my best friend. Sometimes when I'm having a hard time,

I ask him for some help. And when I'm having a good time I say, 'Hey, you scoundrel. You're watching, right?'"

Competition can kill friendships. Greg Moore wasn't having that and became the Pack's magnetic hub. "They took our scooter keys away," Kanaan remembers, "because Greg and I were always racing and locking wheels."

The closeness off the track did not change the drivers' nature on the track. "If anything," says Franchitti, "the friendship heightened our competitiveness." But that didn't mean they couldn't party later, or talk for hours by cell phone when they were countries apart.

And Greg's death left a hole in their hearts.

Kanaan couldn't bring himself to delete Greg's phone number, and now races with a sticker on the back of his helmet that says "I miss you, #99."

Papis says: "When I think about him, I almost have tears in my eyes because it hurts me and it makes me happy at the same time."

But there is an understanding among them. Moore was doing what he was born to do. In a sport that pushes the envelope, tragedy is never far away.

"If you look at champions like Ayrton Senna, who was Greg's idol and mine," Tony Kanaan says, "it looks like special people have a short life. Not all, but some of them. God puts special people here for a while . . . and then He takes them back. I think that's what happened.

"Greg is up there in a better place, and he's laughing big-time. If he was always laughing here, can you imagine him up there?"

The Brat Pack hits Cleveland: (Left to right) Max Papis, Tony Kanaan, Dario Franchitti and Greg.

HI-TECH HEAVEN

Nothing epitomized Greg Moore's jump to the big time better than the move to the Player's garage – a cavernous, state-of-the-art and highly organized working space with a bay for every car and a computer to coax out every performance secret. Suddenly, Gasoline Alley seemed a million miles away.

The on-board computer recorded 50 to 100 items: steering, throttle applications, braking, shifting, whether Greg was riding the clutch... "Combine them with things like speed, engine performance, acceleration," says crew chief Alex Timmermans, "and you can tell if he's having a problem with getting back to full power without spinning a rear tire, or locking brakes. And you can tell what he's attempting to do with the car, which was a lot harder to do when all you had to go on was driver feedback."

that much. Basically, they'd download the information at the track and the crew would take it back for analysis, then exchange information and questions with Greg through an endless stream of cell phone calls.

At first they were slow to utilize the computer to its full capacity. But it soon became a vital part of race preparation.

"Racing is a sport that rewards preparation," Timmermans says. "Those who are able to spend the time and the money up front are better able to prepare driver and car

ble. And Jerry Forsythe provided us with everything we needed."

Not that the human element was taken out of the game. It was simply that Moore had a new crew member who didn't talk much and only spit data. "Rarely would we base a decision solely on Greg's comments or solely on the computer." Timmermans says. "We always used both."

High-tech garage, road crew of 12 to 15, onboard computer — and a chance to drive a million-dollar car. No wonder Greg Moore was

GETAWAY

Celebrities require getaway places — sanctuaries, if you will – where they can slough off the pressure, put the demands on hold and let their batteries recharge. For Ric and Greg Moore, that meant the Sportsmans Club at Rivers Inlet, British Columbia. No TV, no phone lines, no cell phone

service, no cars. Just them, the fish, and the battles for the big ones.

Simon Kelly, whose family owns and runs the lodge, remembers a visit when Greg was about 14.

"They'd had a few sessions when they got skunked and other people came in with big fish. This time they came in with two big ones, over 30 pounds, one in the high 20s. They'd fought them for an hour — *The Old Man and the Sea* stuff — netted them and got them in. I remember their big, beaming smiles." But the competitive spirit

wasn't left behind at the track.

In what would be his final visit, Greg was using light line — 8-pound test on a light fly reel – when he hooked into a 40-pound salmon.

"He fought it into the second hour," Kelly says. "Then the reel seized, literally fell apart. He basically had to hand-line it in. And after two hours, he did. It's still our lodge's light-line fly-rod record."

In the early days it was just Ric and Greg. Later, Greg would sometimes bring some of his buddies.

Of course, no getaway is ever

total. The lodge wasn't big, there were other fishermen there, and in close quarters it never takes long to find out who's who. As Greg's celebrity grew, the questions could be endless.

"Greg would patiently answer them all and be very sincere about it. He enjoyed it," Kelly says. "They'd get their photograph taken with him, and he had time for everybody."

Then, batteries fully charged, he would fly out. The tracks were waiting. There were other fish to fry.

Fishing gear and a photographic memory of the big ones.

LEADER IN THE MAKING

At Greg Moore's memorial service in Maple Ridge, Annie and James Moore, Greg's sister and brother, accepted the checkered flag from the Vancouver Molson Indy, the one he had always dreamed of seeing flash down as he crossed the finish line. That dream wasn't to be. From a racing

standpoint, Vancouver wasn't a lucky place for Greg. But that doesn't mean he wasn't a big winner there. For his hometown fans, it was gratifying to see him develop as a driver, a poised young man of ever-growing popularity, and a significant figure of influence in the driving fraternity.

"Coming into 1999 we'd made changes to the track in response to some concerns," says Stuart Ballantyne, general manager of the Vancouver race. "Now the drivers were concerned that one section was too fast. Kirk Russell of

CART and Scott Pruett, representing the drivers, had a meeting that ended in an impasse.

"We had Greg call Kirk, and 20 minutes later, we had a track. So he had clout. His opinions carried that much weight with CART."

Rena Shanaman, who had watched him since he was 16, never quite got over how quickly he matured, "from the kid with the peach fuzz who'd sit in the corner, rather brash but not speaking up, to somebody who could speak so authoritatively and credibly."

But the kid was always there.

Ballantyne remembers looking for Greg to introduce him to some media people at the track in Toronto. "There he was, doing donuts on his scooter. There's this huge trail of smoke, he's got his foot on the ground, and he's absolutely destroying the rear tire." "When I think about trying to teach drivers to emulate Greg," says Shanaman, who formerly ran the Vancouver race and now is a CART executive, "it's that approachability, that zest for life. He had a special ability to connect with people, no matter what."

Victory eluded him, but the chance to drive in front of the hometown crowd always made the Vancouver Molson Indy a special race and a treasured time for Greg.

RACING HIGHLIGHTS

Two victories, three poles (the first, another of those youngest-in-history honors he seemed to collect), three other trips to the podium, fifth overall in the PPG Cup standings. What words can describe a season like that? How about "disappointing", "frustrating" or "maddening"?

How about all of the above.

For Greg Moore, 1998 was 1997, only more so — rich with promise for half a season, and downhill from there. Half a season in or near the top of the point standings. Half a season of engine failures and accidents — including one in Portland that saw him put on probation and fined $5,000 — as what had looked like a pre-destined PPG Cup victory shriveled and died.

The inside move he made on the 14th lap in Portland saw him carom into Christian Fittipaldi. When the dust settled, Fittipaldi,

Moore, Michael Andretti and Paul Tracy were out of the race. "I went in a little too hot," a chastened Moore said. "It was my mistake, and I'm sorry."

Fittipaldi wasn't impressed. "An apology is good," he said. "But it doesn't change the end result."

Nor could Moore change the end result for his own season. He did rebound two weeks later in Michigan to win his third race and finished second in the finale at Fontana. But his championship dream had seemed so close. After eight races he had been second

and charging. And there he was at the end, failing to finish in seven of the last 11, bouncing from bump to bump, failure to failure.

Nor was it any better in Canada, where the country's expectations applied additional pressure. In Toronto he finished 11th, but at least he finished. In Vancouver, in front of the home folks, another accident put him out after 54 laps.

Time to regroup, to get the old, cool Greg Moore behind the wheel. He even had a slogan. "Fine in '99," he said. "Fine in '99."

Best way to prove you were up close to the podium? Get under the champagne. Winner Alex Zanardi (r), third-place Greg Moore (l) and runner-up Michael Andretti, Gateway 1998

6

A LEGACY OF SPIRIT

Roger Penske caught the racing world by surprise on August 9, 1999, with his announcement in the paddock at Detroit's Belle Isle course. There were no drivers present as he revealed that for the year 2000, Marlboro Team Penske cars would be piloted by Greg Moore and Gil de Ferran.

First place, Miami, 1999.

"When you have that passion and desire to do something that requires risk, part of the exhilaration you get is from being on the edge. It wouldn't be the same if there was not some risk involved." **Driver Ron Fellows**

Al Unser, Jr., Penske's lead driver for the 1999 campaign, would be seeking new opportunities. At that moment, Greg was at the Indianapolis Motor Speedway, where he was racing in the all-star, invitational stock car series known as the International Race of Champions. Even he hadn't known Penske had decided to announce his plans the day before the Detroit Grand Prix. But Greg knew it was coming, as did Tyler Williams, his long-time friend.

On a fishing expedition to Rivers Inlet, British Columbia, one of their favorite escapes, Greg had surprised Williams. "You're looking at the new Marlboro Man," he had proclaimed. "Just keep it hush-hush for about 10 days." He was exhilarated at starting his career anew. Penske, too, was looking for a fresh start. His team had gone more than two years without a win. His announcement upset CART's status quo, involving as it did Unser, scion of a storied American racing family and an accomplished driver in his own right. But it provided Greg Moore with the hope of finally realizing his dreams.

"The fire in Roger's eyes was the big thing," Greg said the next day. "That's really my reason to go there — the intensity Roger has to turn this thing around."

The Moores had been entertaining offers since June 30, the first date possible according to the terms of their contract with Player's/Forsythe. Among the offers they considered were bids from

"*Don't worry about me. I could shake hands with you right now and it wouldn't hurt.*"
**Greg Moore, Fontana,
October 31, 1999**

Team Rahal and Cal Wells. Rahal possessed the Ford-Cosworth motor expected to be the most powerful in 2000; Cal Wells introduced the possibility of an entry into NASCAR, which fascinated Greg and Ric.

Penske could provide even more. "I saw him as a racer, above all," Ric explains. "He might be a billionaire with his business interests, but come race day he was only interested in winning. Some team owners approach racing as another business. Roger's priority is winning."

The Penske contract would make Greg a millionaire. Business opportunities were on the horizon. Still, the accord had more to do with Greg realizing his potential.

"We talked about what his goals and interests were," Penske reflected some months later. "Was he interested in going to Formula One? He thought NASCAR might be the next logical step. We said we'd be willing to give him the opportunity.

"But first Greg wanted to win championships in CART. He made a real commitment to Penske Racing because he agreed to join us without demanding I change to this or that tire, chassis or motor. He had faith in me to do what was necessary. I thought that demonstrated real class."

With the news out, Moore's friends witnessed a turnaround in his optimism. "It was huge," Franchitti reflects, "Greg was like a kid with a new toy. He was finally going to get the chance to

"Watching him qualify at Homestead both years, he was on the pole and very impressive. You have no idea what it is to go flat around one of those turns. It's very, very difficult. I don't care how good the car is, it's a feat, and as a driver I can appreciate it better than anybody else." **Gil de Ferran**

When drivers meet, they talk cars, and the ones on the way up are forever gleaning knowledge from the ones already there. Greg Moore and Patrick Carpentier (r) spend some quality time with Al Unser Jr.

show what he could do on all kinds of circuits — as well as the ovals where he felt he was pretty well unbeatable, which was pretty much the case."

The mood at Player's/Forsythe was fragile from the beginning of 1999. That tension eased with initial success. Coming out of Homestead with the best result to date — a maximum 22 points for winning, qualifying on the pole and leading the most laps – Greg was atop the driver standings. He stayed there through a subsequent fourth place finish at Japan, where he recovered from a spin on the second to last lap to cross the finish line with fraying tires. He achieved an eighth place finish at Long Beach.

Yet, as the summer heated up, the results increasingly belied the motto that had sustained the Moores' five-year plan: All Will Be Fine in '99. Greg put together top-10 results through another four starts, culminating with a second behind Paul Tracy at Milwaukee. But in 10 of the season's last 13 races, car number 99 was to finish out of the points.

A crash eliminated him from the Vancouver race, as one of many drivers skidding on the rain-slicked streets into the unforgiving walls. It was his third consecutive year of failing to finish his hometown contest as a result of contact. "Dad, do you think we could just take a bye in Vancouver?" he sheepishly kidded Ric.

Greg was sustained not only by his belief in Marlboro Team Penske for 2000, but by a conviction that there was one last race he could hope to win for Player's/Forsythe.

He was extremely close to team owner Jerry Forsythe. Winning one more race for Forsythe, and for his crew, many of whom had been with him for years, would salvage the year.

The Marlboro 500 at Fontana, California, on October 31, offered $1 million for first place, but, more enticing to Greg than that, the two-mile, high-banked oval was one venue where his Reynard Mercedes was the equal of any car.

In opening practice on Friday, Moore was only 18th, with a best-lap average of 230.685 mph. He wasn't concerned. "We did pretty good but the wind was nasty," he said. "This is a long race and we have to be sure that everything on the car is in perfect order. The Player's team mainly worked on race set-up today." *(continued on page 124)*

"The thing I keep going back to is his passion. He had a passion for his friends and he had a passion for life. He was always smiling. The lesson to be learned is that he taught us to be passionate, to love and not to waste a single day of your life. Everybody knows he was one hell of a race car driver, and ten times a human being." Jimmy Vasser

*Above left: Behind bars with Juan Montoya (l) and Tony Kanaan (r) at the Alcatraz restaurant in
San Francisco. Above right: Taking stock in Hollywood. Below right: Floor hockey with Patrick Carpentier.
Below left: Checking out the Big Apple. Sometimes it seemed the laughter would never end.*

The pit crew — heroes in the trenches. "The pit stops now mean more than ever," says Dario Franchitti's chief mechanic, Kyle Moyer. "A few years ago I felt like our team had a pretty good advantage because we put a lot of importance in them and not many others did. But now everybody concentrates really hard on them."

It looked for a while as though Greg might get away with flipping the bird at Juan Montoya for cutting him off in the 1999 U.S. 500 at Michigan Speedway. Officials missed the incident until they saw it pictured in newspapers. Then they fined Moore $5,000.

A long way from the track, Greg takes advantage of a rare day off while in Florida.

*Greg Moore's face
has graced the covers of
racing magazines around
the world.*

"COPY!"

The first time he heard Greg Moore say it, Jason Priestley thought "Weird!" After he'd heard it 20 times, he knew he had to steal it. One word: "Copy!" They were fast friends by then, two guys from Vancouver

who shared a love of cars and racing. Priestley was a TV star, Brandon on *Beverly Hills 90210.* Moore, six years younger, was flirting with greatness. They met, they clicked, and they spent as much time together as schedules allowed.

And every time Jason said something, Greg would reply "Copy!"

"He finally told me it was what he said all the time in the car answering the crew over his radio. Like, 'Copy this, copy that,'" Priestley explains. "And I said, 'Oh, dude, can I steal that?'

"'You can have it,' he said, and I told him I'd use it on the show."

Brandon was going to say "Copy?" because his pal said it?

"I don't believe you!" said Greg.

"Wait!" said Priestley. And one night he phoned. "Wednesday night at 8 p.m., you'll hear me say 'Copy.'"

"He said, 'I don't believe you,'" Priestley laughs. "But after the show he called and said, 'Dude, I can't believe you did that. But I'm really glad you did because I invited all the boys over to hear it, and if you hadn't, I'd have been in soooo much trouble!'"

For five years they shared worries and troubles, laughter and dreams. The last call came at 5 a.m., just before the final trip to Fontana.

"I was in New York," Priestley recalls. "He was driving up to the lake to go fishing. He said I was the only guy he knew who'd be up, and we talked until he got out of the car to fish. I wished him good luck Sunday and said I'd talk to him after the race.

"I so looked forward to knowing him as a 30-year-old man, and as a 40-year-old, and as a father and husband."

Dario Franchitti, Jason Priestley, Greg and Tammy Gaskell.

Behind the scenes, the action seldom stops. Above right: Greg and fellow-Canadian Paul Tracy
grab a few moments conversation before jumping back into the media mix.
Below right: Greg surveys the damage after parking his car under Scott Pruett's in Detroit.

Next morning Greg was riding his scooter through the paddock when a woman in a pick-up truck turned in front of him. "She just hit my rear wheel," he told reporters. "If I hadn't accelerated, she probably would have got me in the leg and I wouldn't be standing here right now, that's for sure."

Greg suffered a broken bone in his right hand, lacerations to his fingers and a scraped right hip. Although he missed qualifying, CART, after consulting with doctors, ruled he could start the race from last place, 26th. Ric and Donna were with him inside the medical center as 15 stitches went into his little finger and ring finger. "He was very queasy during the stitches," said his stepmother, "but when it was done he sort of popped up and said, 'Well, what about tomorrow?'"

Three laps running alone on the track at the end of the day satisfied any personal doubt about his ability to steer with his injured hand encased in a mitt-

Ric tends to Greg's injured hand prior to the Fontana race.

like, modified glove. "I'll be fine," he told reporters who persisted in asking how he could expect to steer at 230 mph. "I'm a tough Canadian kid. We're used to playing hurt."

Those close to him sensed his growing will. Put your head down and go for it. This time it would be all the more of a challenge and he relished the prospect.

To his girlfriend, Greg minimized what had happened. "He had told me on the phone he had

a little fall," said Tammy Gaskell. "When I arrived and saw him I was shocked because he'd totally downplayed it."

Roger Penske dropped by the motor home Saturday evening. Donna Moore had offered to make dinner for Greg only to find his refrigerator barren of anything but scraps. She'd mixed every kind of pasta, an assortment of sauces from near-empty jars and whatever vegetables were still edible. As Greg chowed down, she wondered if Penske would think this was typical of her cooking.

But Penske only noticed a fully charged future employee. "We just talked about how he was ready to go," Penske remembers. "He was smiling from ear to ear, glowing at the opportunities."

For the moment, Greg Moore wasn't thinking ahead to giving Roger Penske his 100th CART win in the year 2000. Now, Greg's focus was entirely on Sunday's race.

Greg's sister Annie telephoned Sunday morning. She called to say she thought he shouldn't race, and that she loved him. Donna, who answered the phone, told her daughter there was no point in telling Greg he shouldn't run — he was determined to compete. When Greg heard Annie had said to tell him she loved him, he exclaimed, "Oh, that's so cool! She never said that before."

Max Papis saw Greg Sunday morning.

Facing page: Marlboro 500, California Speedway, Fontana, October 31, 1999.

A dream not to be: Photo of his test drive for Roger Penske and the helmet and suit Greg Moore was to wear in 2000 when he joined the Penske team.

"He said, 'Hey, wait for me, I'm coming up,'" Papis relates. "'Are you strong enough?' I asked, and he said, 'Strong enough to kick your ass.'"

The kidding continued as the drivers were introduced to the crowd, one by one. "Greg, you've got to take a cab to your car," Tony Kanaan joked. "Hey, just wait for me," Greg retorted. "Give me some room on the outside. I'll be right in your tow on the second lap."

"I started 10th," says Kanaan, "and I did look in my mirror on the second lap. The guy was two cars behind me."

Greg charged hard, without reservation, passing high, passing low. This was to be a 500-mile race, but the Canadian's mission appeared to be reaching his rightful place at the front of the pack within 50 miles.

On the fourth lap American Richie Hearn lost control coming out of turn two and spun into the inside wall. His car broke apart on impact, as race cars are designed to do, dissipating energy to prevent injury to the driver. Hearn walked away.

After five slow laps behind the pace car while wreckage was cleared, racing resumed. Now Greg was on the move again, up to full race velocity. Then, without warning, at almost the same point as Hearn, his car lost its grip.

It spun wildly, carrying him off the track at a different angle than Hearn. Crossing the slick infield grass the car became airborne and crashed hard into the retaining wall.

Greg took the brunt of the hit. At the point of impact the force was 154 G's, the highest ever measured by a CART crash data sensor.

The race continued. The drivers were not told of Moore's death until after the checkered flag had marked Adrian Fernandez the winner. There were tears, so many tears, among the drivers and reporters — everyone who had believed Greg's future was limitless.

"I thought it was another car [that had crashed]," said a sobbing Max Papis, who'd finished second. "It never touched my mind. I never thought it might be Greg."

"He was the guy I competed with the hardest on the track, and he was the guy I had the most fun with away from the track. The guy was going to be a champion many times over." A crew member tries to

You have left us with tears in our hearts, but smiles in our memories.

Max Papis

Jennifer
Haug

Ms. Richards
Class

to:
Greg

Moore

Dreams
never
end.

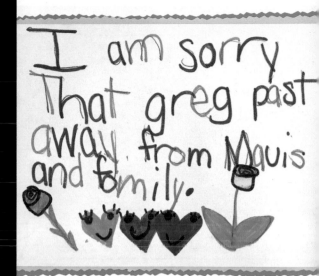

I am sorry
That greg past
away from Mauis
and family.

Greg Moore you
Where NumBer
CHELSEA
MS.

MOOBE

Greg
#1

Greg Moore was
Much more than a
very, very, talented
Cart Racing Driver
Smart, funny, caring
and much, Much
more. I will always
Remember Greg Moore
Robert
Williams

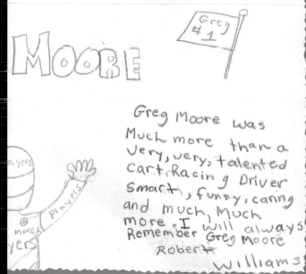

Cards, letters, flowers — words of sympathy and a shared grief flooded from around the world into the house in Maple Ridge. Nowhere was it better expressed than in the simple words and drawings of

A BROTHER'S FAREWELL

The following is taken from the eulogy delivered by James Moore at his brother Greg's memorial service at St. Andrew's Wesley United Church, Vancouver, British Columbia, November 3, 1999. "I'd like to thank you all for attending the service today. This is one party that Greg wouldn't have missed

for the world. In fact, I think that might be an understatement.

Because we can all picture it now: People standing around, mingling, having a decent time. And then, a deafening screech as a black Dodge Viper comes ripping around the corner and lays down enough rubber to make Alex Zanardi's donuts seem like child's play.

The driver's door opens. A young man gets out. He looks cool, smooth, and dignified, and he knows it. After all, he did spend an hour in the bathroom on his hair alone.

The doors swing open and our guy walks in, each stride catching someone's attention. He has changed the face of the party for the better, even if his shoes do look like he just got laid off by Barnum & Bailey.

That was his effect on people. He was fun, and even funny occasionally, and he was the people's champion, which is why thousands of people feel the same way I do today: They have lost something near and dear to their hearts.

Greg wasn't just Ric Moore's boy. He was also Maple Ridge's boy, British Columbia's boy, and Canada's boy . . .

Ah, there are so many good times, I can't even begin to include half of them. But I do want to accomplish something.

In all the years I've known Greg, not once did I ever say, "Greg, I love you. You're my best friend."

It seems that I always took our relationship for granted, and this is my only regret. So now I would like to make up for it while Greg is listening.

Greg, you are an awesome brother, a fantastic friend, and a noble adversary. Pass Ayrton once on the outside for me. I love you."

Greg with James and Annie.

GIVING BACK

In the days when the Greg Moore team was a father-funded, family-run dream, and the money was all but gone, Mike Hurst can remember Ric knocking on a lot of corporate doors and making a simple plea: "Let's not let this kid fail because he doesn't have the money. If he fails, let it be because he

doesn't have the talent or loses interest. But not because the money isn't there. Someone opened a door for you. Help us open one for him."

Enough people listened — and Greg Moore never forgot.

He understood that with that help came an obligation, a trust, to help others in turn. And, being Greg Moore, he jumped in with both feet.

He was the first Canadian spokesman for the Molson's *Take Care* safe driving campaign. He carried the message to a dozen Canadian colleges in 18 months,

squeezing campus visits into his madcap schedule. To promote a take-transit campaign, he drove a bus around the Vancouver Indy site.

He lent his name, his time, and his effort to five charities: the Kidney Foundation of British Columbia, the Vancouver and Ridge Meadows hospital foundations, the Juvenile Diabetes Foundation, and the British Columbia Brain Injury Association. Whenever and wherever he could, he stepped in to help, from public appearances where his name and face might help to open hearts and wallets to a smile and a

handshake and an encouraging "Cool! Keep it up. You'll get it done" to those in need.

It wasn't about celebrity or showmanship. Greg Moore was saying "Thank you," and it gave him a special joy.

His work for the five charities will be carried on by the Greg Moore Foundation. It will present scholarships to the schools attended by Greg, James and Annie. And there will be aid for young athletes who lack the timely financial boost that could open the door that vital crack. As it did for him.

Supporting charitable causes was a high priority with Greg, shown here with representatives of the five major causes he supported, as well as the Swan-e-set Bay Resort and Country Club, host of the Greg Moore Pro-Am golf tournament.

EPILOGUE

Greg Moore's signature red gloves.
Facing page: Max Papis wins the first race of the 2000
season, and dedicates it to his departed friend.

Max Papis's first win on the CART circuit came on March 26, 2000, at Homestead-Miami Speedway. It was at this race on this course that everyone within the racing community knew that Greg Moore had anticipated giving Roger Penske his 100th victory.

Recognizing his mastery of this 1.5-mile oval, it seemed natural that he would deliver. His record at Homestead made the case.

Instead, the fiery, ebullient Papis won and dedicated the win to his close friend. Almost five months had passed since the day in Fontana, California. In every interview since then, Papis had said that Greg, for him, would live forever. And he surely did at this moment.

Papis's voice first addressed his crew while on his cool-down lap. "Hey guys, we made it, thank you." Then, "Greg, I love you."

The joy on the victory podium was something to behold. Roberto Moreno, the diminutive Brazilian who had finished second, found himself hoisted on to the victor's shoulder. Paul Tracy, third, doused Papis with champagne before hugging him.

"Today was very special," Papis said. Asked to explain further, he said only, "I want to keep those thoughts to myself. Ric, you know what I mean.

"The strongest feeling I am going to keep for me — and my friend knows what I feel."

His last comment was to mystify some onlookers. "Red gloves rule," Max Papis said, "Red gloves rule."

Some drivers wear white gloves, some blue, some the color of their driving suit. Max Papis wears red gloves. Greg Moore wore red gloves. In Papis's mind, Greg Moore always will wear red gloves and his friend's legacy of spirit will remain equally as vivid.

FATHER *and* SON

Around the time Greg was turning 12 he was already a very good athlete in hockey and kicking some pretty serious butt in karting. I decided instead of a birthday card I wanted to write him a letter.

Now, I'm not much of a letter writer, but I wanted to do this one. The letter basically said, "Greg, you are a very good athlete and a very good driver, but what you always have to remember is, it was the luck of the draw that God gave you the ability to do that. You're not a better person than anyone else. You are luckier." Greg and I had a lot of time to talk with each other. I'm glad we did. I was able to present issues to him that I thought were important. I'm lucky that Greg could handle the issues and respond. I never had the chance to have those kinds of talks with my dad. I didn't want to miss the chance with Greg.

In 1994, after Greg won in Indy Lights for the first time, I thought the time was right for a conversation I had been thinking about for some time.

Ric and two-year-old Greg on Canim Lake, B.C.
Facing page: The pre-race ritual, a handshake from Dad.

"Son, we need to have a meeting. Sit down for a minute."

"What for?" Greg said, confused.

"I want you to decide what kind of a person you're going to be."

His future looked bright. It was time he decided if he would become a jerk — and the world already had too many jerks — or if he was going to stay the way he was: a nice guy.

We used Wayne Gretzky as an example. One of the nicest guys, one of the hardest workers, he represented his sport really well and still became the top guy. He'd take time to sign autographs and talk with kids. I believe the truly great people always do that.

I said to Greg, "The reporter who asks you a question on Sunday afternoon doesn't know you've already answered it 50 times. It may sound really stupid to you, but you have to make sure you listen to him."

And it became his decision: "Why change?" he thought. And he didn't.

RIC MOORE

So far, so good!

PLAYER'S LTD.

PLAYER'S LTÉE

PLAYER'S RACING

INDECK PLAYER'S

PLAYER'S RACING TEAM

99-003
COMPETITION LICENCE
Name of Holder: Greg Moore
Type: DRIVER-RACE
Category & Grade: International A
Issue Date: January 1, 1999
December 31, 1999

championship
drivers
association, inc.
Greg Moore

28 — MOTOR SPORTS

CART STAR GREG MOORE KILLED IN FONTANA SEASON FINALE

OnTrack
Auto Racing Magazine of Record

GREG MOORE
APRIL 22, 1975 – OCT. 31, 1999

Greg Moore

GREG MO
IndyLights

INDY L

Greg Moore: Year-by-Year

1985

Started racing karts, age 10.

1989

Won North American Enduro Kart Championship, age 14.

1990

Repeated as North American Enduro Kart Champion & started racing Formula Ford cars, winning the Spenard David Racing School competition at Shannonville, Ontario.

1991

Esso Protec Formula Ford 1600 Rookie of the Year and fourth in overall championship with one win, four seconds, and two pole positions.

1992

USAC Formula 2000 West Champion and Rookie of the Year.

Won four races, took four poles.

1993

Moved up to Indy Lights championship circuit, driving for small family team run by father Ric.

Best race in rookie Lights season was at the Portland, Oregon, road course in June where he qualified fifth and finished third. Greg always considered Portland one of his home tracks, racing there from the start of his career in karts.

Best qualifying effort in rookie Lights season was on the Milwaukee Mile oval, where he qualified second and finished fifth.

Ranked ninth in 1993 Lights championship.

1994

Continued with family team and won the Indy Lights season-opener at Phoenix in April.

At 18, Greg became the youngest driver ever to win a CART-sanctioned race. He went on to win two more Lights races in 1994 at New Hampshire in August and Nazareth in September. All three victories came on oval tracks.

Greg scored nine top-five finishes in 12 races and qualified in the top 10 for every race. He finished third in the championship behind Englishman Steve Robertson and Brazilian Andre Ribeiro, beating former motorcycle World Champion Eddie Lawson, who finished fourth.

1995

Joined Jerry Forsythe's Player's team to drive in Indy Lights, signing a five-year contract intended to take him into Indy cars. This was Greg's first contract with a professional team, aged only 18 when the contract was signed.

Responded in magnificent style, winning the 1995 Indy Lights Championship with a spectacular, record-setting season. He took seven poles and won 10 of 12 races, including the first five of the year in a row.

Set a Lights point record of 242 - 30 more than any previous champion. Won the championship by 102 points, led 375 laps, and finished every lap of every race.

1996

Graduated to Indy cars at 20 years of age.

Qualified sixth and finished seventh in first CART Champ car race at Homestead-Miami Speedway in March. Impressed observers by coming back from a stop-and-go pit

Westwood Jr. Stock, first place, 1986.

Portland, Grand National Champion, Kart-O-Rama junior class, 1990.

USAC F-2000 Championship West, champion driver, 1992.

Firestone Indy Lights Championship, first place, 1994.

lane violation penalty, which cost him a lap, passing race winner Jimmy Vasser, on his way to seventh place.

Led second CART race of career in Brazil two weeks later before experiencing mechanical trouble

Finished third in Australia in next race, then took spectacular second place at Nazareth at the end of April behind Michael Andretti, beating Al Unser Jr., Emerson Fittipaldi, Paul Tracy, Bobby Rahal, and Jimmy Vasser.

Scored one more podium finish that year: third place at Cleveland in July behind Gil de Ferran and Jimmy Vasser.

Finished ninth in championship. Led 73 laps.

Second in Rookie-of-the-Year standings to Alex Zanardi.

1997

Scored first CART victory at Milwaukee in June to become the youngest driver in the history of American National Championship, or Indy car racing, to win a race, aged 22 years 1 month and 10 days.

Won again in Detroit the next weekend beating Michael Andretti, Gil de Ferran, and Jimmy Vasser.

Finished second three times: to Scott Pruett at Surfers Paradise in Australia in April, to Paul Tracy at Rio de Janeiro in May, and to Alex Zanardi at Mid-Ohio in August.

Qualified in top 10 in 15 of 17 races.

Finished seventh in championship and led 142 laps.

1998

Qualified on the pole and finished second to Michael Andretti and ahead of Alex Zanardi in season opener on Homestead-Miami oval.

Won in Rio de Janeiro in May, beating Zanardi and Adrian Fernandez.

Qualified on pole at Gateway Raceway two weeks later and finished third behind Zanardi and Michael Andretti.

Qualified second at Milwaukee and took pole at Detroit in June.

Beat Jimmy Vasser and Alex Zanardi in spectacular last lap shoot-out in July's U.S. 500 at Michigan, a race that featured a record 62 lead changes.

Took pole in inaugural Houston street race in October and finished second to Vasser and ahead of Zanardi in fierce season-closing 500-mile race at California Speedway.

Led 11 races and led the championship after rounds four and five at Nazareth and Rio.

Finished fifth in championship points. Highest-scoring driver in oval races with 113 points.

Led a total of 251 laps.

1999

Took fifth pole and fifth win of career in season-opener at Homestead-Miami Speedway. Led 96 of 150 laps, beating Michael Andretti by 1.1 seconds with Dario Franchitti third.

Bounced back from big crash in practice to finish fourth in second round at Motegi, Japan, after crossing the finish line backwards following a thrown tire tread.

Led the championship after the first three races. Finished second to Paul Tracy at Milwaukee in June and third in Detroit in August behind Franchitti and Tracy.

Experienced mechanical trouble in five of last six races of year, falling down championship table.

Signed three-year contract in August to drive for Roger Penske in 2000-2002.

Killed while coming through the field in the season-closing 500-mile race at the California Speedway.

Career Totals

Started 72 CART Indy car races ■ *Five wins, including one 500-mile win (1998 U.S. 500).*
Twelve other podium finishes (second or third) ■ *Won five poles* ■ *Led 568 laps.*

Miller 200 Milwaukee Mile, first win, 1997.   *Detroit Grand Prix, Belle Isle, first place, 1997.*   *Grand Prix of Brazil champion, 1998.*   *Grand Prix of Miami, Homestead, first place, 1999.*

ACKNOWLEDGEMENTS

James, Greg and Annie Moore.

Inspero Productions

Publishing Director: Marthe Love
Editorial Director: Arthur Pincus
Creative Director: Judy Rudin
Authors: Dan Proudfoot, Gordon Kirby
with Jim Taylor
Senior Designer: John Belisle/CDDC
Editor: Brian Scrivener

Corporate Sales: Mike Hurst,
Glenn McPherson
Publishing Coordinator: Robin Evans
Photo Editor: Brian Daisley
Design Assistant: Belinda Waeland/CDDC
Production: Chris Robertson/CDDC

Photo Coordination: Ryan Baggott, Penelope
Bridge, Galen Curnoe, Lisa Morrison, Tallulah,
Frank Vena, Milan Vertone, Brynn Wanstall
Executive Assistant: Cynthia Langan/CDDC
Proofreading: Karen Love
Indexing: Cathy Love

*Inspero Productions would like to extend a special thank you to the Moore family and the Greg Moore Foundation,
especially Mr. and Mrs. Ric Moore, in appreciation of all their cooperation and support.*

The Greg Moore Foundation would like to acknowledge the following for their financial assistance and support:
Don Brown, Players Racing • Gerald Forsythe • Steve Potter, Mercedes-Benz, USA •
Al Speyer, Bridgestone/Firestone • Bill Simpson, Simpson Safety Equipment •

General Acknowledgements

Stephen Adams • Cary Agaginian • Bruce Allen • Mario Andretti • Roger Bailey • Pieter Baljet • Stuart Ballantyne • Lindsey Barr • Estella Bekessey • David Benefield • Lee Bentham • Randy Berswick • Kate Bird • Tom Blattler • Edward Bonjonia • Ezio Bortoluzzi • Susan Bradshaw • Steve Brody • Tony Brunetti • Michael Burch, Robert McCullough, Whitecap Books • Chris Bye • Francois Cartier • Steve and Tracey Challis • David Coulthard • David Counsell • Crusher • Ian Cunningham • Tina Dale • Cheryl Day Anderson • Gil de Ferran • Dr. Jacques Delaire • Rosko Dickenson • Gerry Donaldson • Tanya Embree • David Empringham • Ron Fellows • Adrian Fernandez • Christian Fittipaldi • Dario Franchitti • Jeri Gargano, ASAP Sports • Tammy Gaskell • Mark Green • John Gorsline • Janet Grove • Charlie Hall • Amber Hamilton • Norbert Haug • Matthew Hayes • Paul Hayes • Brian Hellevang • Graham Hookey • Trevor Hoskins • Kent Holden • Barry Houlihan • Mike Hurst • Mario Illien • Darryl and Kathy Issa • Jay Ivey • Mark and Ali James • Paul Kariya • Tony Kanaan • Simon Kelly • Rick Klein • Jules Kopinski • Troy Lee • Reimut Leider • Jim Longridge • Douglas Love • Jennifer Love • Dan Luginbuhl • Gary Mason • Jergen Mathias • Woody McMilllin • Neil Micklewright • Alan Mille • Annie Moore • Mrs. Donna Moore • James Moore • Paul Morgan • Tony Morris • Brendan Morrison • Mike and Anne Murphy • Devin and Taylor Murray • Kevin Oake • Dr. Steve Olvey • Peter Orlowsky • Max Papis • Gabriele Pedone • Roger Penske • Ellen Pincus • Jason Priestley • Lorne Priestley • Bobby Rahal • Alan Robbie • Jorge Rocha • Kirk Russell • Adam Saal • Steve Shoellhorn • Joe Siano • Barb and Jay Signore • Rena Shanaman • Richard Spenard • Paul and Monika Strak • Scott Steele • Jackie Stewart • Brad Thomas • Mark Thorne • Alex Timmermans • Paul Tracy • Dr. Terry Trammell • Robert Turner • Garry Valk • Tammy Valkosky • Clint Van Blanken • Jimmy Vasser • Jacques Villeneuve • Allen Wayne • Justin Weiss, Allsport Photography • Leroy White • Carol Wilkins • Tyler Williams • John Winter • Alex Zanardi • David and Janice Zimmerly •

The Greg Moore Foundation and Inspero Productions would like to thank the following for the generous donation of their photographs:

David Ashlock, Bridgestone/Firestone • Pieter Baljet • Amanda Bates • Bill Bauman • Allen Beaulieu • Michael C. Brown • Peter Burke • *Champ Car* • Mike Cole, The Raceworks • Cheryl Day Anderson • *Extreme Magazine* • Gerry Frechette, Rainbow

Action Photography • Tammy Gaskell • Amber Hamilton • Phil Hietanen • *Inside Track Motorsport News* • Simon Kelly • Robert Kerian • Nelson Machin • Michael Levitt • Ryker Lomas • Andrew Malion • *Maple Ridge News* • Mercedes

Benz USA • Guy Motil • Kim Noble • *On Track Auto Racing Magazine* • Player's Library • *The Province* • *Racer* • *Sports Only* • *TV Week* • *The Vancouver Sun* • Alex Waterhouse Hayward • Paul Webb • Leroy White •

CREDITS

Photo Credits

Cover: Chris Relke

Ashlock, David, Bridgestone/Firestone: 130 row two left; Baljet, Pieter: 52 below right; Bates, Amanda: 133; Bauman, Bill: 138 above right; Beaulieu, Allen: 136; Boyd, Dan R.: 14 above, 25, 29 right, 63 above left, 63 below right, 65, 88, 89,101 above left, 101 centre left, 101 below left, 101 below right, 105 below right, 114 above, 124, 138 below right; Brown, Michael C.: 2, 6, 17 above right, 21, 73 below right, 114 below left, 129, back endsheets; Brown, Michael C./*Champ Car* : 121, 139; Burke, Peter: 130 row two centre; Chin, Phillip/*TV Week*: 11; Cole, Mike/The Raceworks: 37 below left, 47; Danforth , Perry: 8-9, 22, 31, 39 above left, 39 below left, 40, 46, 49, 57 above left, 57 below left, 58, 67, 77 above left, 77 below left, 78, 87, 96, 97 above left, 97 below left, 100, 106, 111, 126, 135, 138-139, 140-141; Day Anderson, Cheryl: 4, 5, 14 below, 52 above right, 57 below right, 59 above, 93 below left, 97 above right, 97 below right, 118 above, 122 above left, 139 centre right; diZinno, Tony: 61; Eisberg, Jon: front endsheets, 10, 66, 79, 85, 99; Ferrey, Jon/Allsport Photography: 119; Frechette, Gerry/Rainbow Action Photography: 56, 57 above right; Gaskell, Tammy: 117 above left, 117 above right, 117 below left, 121; Grassman, Don/*Racer*: 121; Hamilton, Amber: 77 above right; Hathaway, Barry/Allsport Photography/*Racer*: 121, 138; Hawkins, Stephen: 93 above right; Hietanen, Phil: 39 above right; Hodge, Craig/*The Vancouver Sun*: 27 above left; Kelly, Simon: 107 below left, 107 below right; Kerian, Robert: 109, 112, 113, 114 below right, 115, 123, 130 row three centre; LaBerge, Robert/Allsport Photography: 81, 103, 110, 120, 130 row one right, 130 row four right, 134; © leRoi/White, LeRoi, B.: 70 below; Levitt, Michael: 13, 23, 28, 29 left, 77 below, 94, 95 below, 104, 108, 118 below, 130 row three left; Lindsay, Ian/*The Vancouver Sun*: 62; Lomas, Ryker: 93 above left; Machin, Nelson: 15; Malion, Andrew: 73 above left, 138 above right; Courtesy Mercedes-Benz USA: 12, 83, 93 below right, 122 below right,130 row one centre; Moore, Donna, Mrs.: 32, 35, 37 above left, 41, 42, 52 above left, 137; Moore, Ric & Donna: 8-9, 30, 34, 37 above right, 37 below right, 38, 43, 44, 51, 52 below left, 53, 63 above right, 63 below left, 84, 107 above left, 107 above right, 130 row four centre, 132; Motil, Guy: 127; Noble, Kim: 70 above; Papis, Max: 95 above; Courtesy of the Player's Library: 98 above, 98 below right, 105 above left, 105 above right, 105 below left, 122 above right, 130 row one left, 130 row three right; Player's Library/*Extreme Magazine*: 11; Powell, Mike/Allsport Photography: 17 above left; Price, Colin/*The Province*, 26, 27 above right, 138 centre; Relke, Chris: cover, 20, 27 below left; Relke, Chris/*The Province*, 117 below right; Relke, Chris/Sports Only: 139 above left; Rondeau, Pascal/Allsport Photography: 17 below left,143; Russell, Chuck/*The Province*, 27 below right; Smith, Dale/*Maple Ridge News*: 9, below left, 50; Squire, Jamie/Allsport Photography: 68, 69, 71, 73 below left, 91, 101 above right, 101 centre right, 122 below left, back single endsheet, back cover; Stines, Rod/*On Track Auto Racing Magazine*: 121, 139 below right; Strak, Paul/Gridwork Photography: 45, 55, 59 below, 64, 82, 98 below left, 138 above left; Strak, Paul/Gridwork Photography/ *Inside Track Motorsport News*: 121; Swope, Steve: front single endsheet, 18-19, 86, 90 below; Taylor, David/Allsport Photography: 29 centre, 76, 90 above, 130 row four left; Waterhouse Hayward, Alex: 8 above left, 39 below right, 48, 142; Webb, Paul: 3, 17 below right, 73 above right, 74-75, 125, 130 row two right.

Artifact Credits

The Greg Moore Foundation and Inspero Productions would like to thank the following individuals and institutions for their generous assistance in allowing access to their artifacts and memorabilia:

Ric and Donna Moore, Mrs. Donna Moore, Amber Hamilton, Andrew Malion, Kimberly Noble, Edith McDermott Elementary School students, West Heights Elementary School students.

Select Bibliography

The Greg Moore Foundation and Inspero Productions wish to thank the following publications for certain interview and background material used in producing this book:

Autosport, November 11, 1999; *Champ Car*, Season Preview 1999; *Championship Racing Magazine*, December 1999; *Extreme Magazine*, Summer 1996; *The Indianapolis Star*; *Inside Track Motorsport News*, December 10, 1999; *Maclean's*, November 15, 1999 and December 20, 1999; *On Track Auto Racing Magazine*, November 18, 1999, December 2, 1999 and December 30, 1999; *Performance Racing News*, January 2000; *Racer*, September 1997, November 1999, December 1999 and January 2000; *Stars & Cars*, Winter 1997; *TV Week*, August 31 – September 6, 1996; *The Vancouver Sun*.

INDEX